Cocos2D Game Development Essentials

Bring your mobile game ideas to life with Cocos2D

Ben Trengrove

BIRMINGHAM - MUMBAI

Cocos2D Game Development Essentials

First published: January 2015

Production reference: 1190115

Published by Packt Publishing Ltd.
Livery Place
35 Livery Street
Birmingham B3 2PB, UK.

ISBN 978-1-78439-032-7

www.packtpub.com

Cover image by Ben Trengrove (ben@nybbles.com.au)

Credits

Author
Ben Trengrove

Reviewers
K. Aava Rani

Sergio Martínez-Losa Del Rincón

Allen Sherrod

Commissioning Editor
Akram Hussain

Acquisition Editor
Richard Gall

Content Development Editor
Poonam Jain

Technical Editor
Parag Topre

Copy Editor
Relin Hedly

Project Coordinator
Mary Alex

Proofreaders
Simran Bhogal

Linda Morris

Indexer
Mariammal Chettiyar

Graphics
Abhinash Sahu

Production Coordinator
Alwin Roy

Cover Work
Alwin Roy

About the Author

Ben Trengrove is an experienced iOS developer who started developing with the release of the first iOS SDK. He spent 3 years as the senior developer at Shiny Things (`http://getshinythings.com`), where he lead the creation of all Shiny Things games using Cocos2d. These apps have been featured as the editor's choice by Apple around the world. Today, Ben runs a mobile app agency that is based out of Canberra, Australia—Stripy Sock (`http://stripysock.com.au`).

I would like to thank my gorgeous wife for her patience during several weekends that I spent writing.

About the Reviewers

K. Aava Rani is the cofounder of CulpzLab Pvt Ltd, a software company, with 10 years of experience in game technologies. A successful blogger and a technologist, she switched her focus to game development in the year 2004. Since then, she has produced a number of game titles and has provided art and programming solutions to Unity developers across the globe. She is based in New Delhi, India. Aava Rani has been the recipient of several prestigious awards, including Adobe for Game Technology Expert 2012 and SmartFoxServer, for her articles. She has immense experience in different technologies and has reviewed *Creating E-learning games with Unity3D*, *Packt Publishing*.

Founded in 2010, CulpzLab has proven itself to be a reliable technology partner for its clients. Currently, CulpzLab employs over 50 people and has its office based out of New Delhi in India. CulpzLab is a leading-edge custom-process-driven software solutions provider that has helped and partnered with many reputed brands, start-up ventures, and offshore IT companies. It has helped them realize and deliver effective, efficient, and on-time digital solutions. Thanks to its diverse technology background, industry expertise, and a client footprint that extends to more than 14 countries, CulpzLab has worked with a plethora of clients on a global platform. It is well positioned to help organizations derive maximum value from their IT investments and fully support their business aims. CulpzLab's core business purpose is to invent, engineer, and deliver technology solutions that drive business value, create social value, and improve the lives of customers.

I would like to acknowledge the creators of Unity3D program, an amazing tool that allows ultimate digital experience and creative expression. I'd also like to thank my clients for being part of the fun! Many of you have become good friends through my creative successes. Finally, I'd like to thank R.K.Rajanjan who taught me how to fall in love with technologies.

Sergio Martínez-Losa Del Rincón is a computer engineer. He was fond of programming languages since his high school days, when he learned programming and computer interaction. He is always learning and discovering something new everyday.

He likes all kinds of programming languages, but his main area of focus is mobile development with native languages, such as Objective-C (iPhone), Java (Android), and Xamarin (C#). He also builds Google Glass applications, as well as mobile applications for iPhone and Android devices. Sergio also develops games for mobile devices with Cocos2d-x and Cocos2d. He also likes cross-platform applications and has reviewed *Learning Xamarin Studio, Packt Publishing*.

Sergio loves challenging problems and is always keen to work with new technologies. Visit www.linkedin.com/in/sergiomtzlosa for more details and information about his experiences.

Allen Sherrod is a lifelong gamer with a passion for programming and video game development, which he has been involved in for the past 10 years. When he is not helping people run raids on Destiny (video game) developed by Bungie, he is working hard by programming various tools and mobile video game applications. Currently, Allen is a mobile software engineer at Disney Interactive, which is one of the best companies to work for. He has also reviewed books such as *Instant New iPad Features in iOS 6 How-to* and *Instant Apple iBooks How-to, Packt Publishing*.

I'd like to thank Packt Publishing for giving me the opportunity to review this title. I would also like to thank the author for doing a great job in putting together this book. Book writing is no easy task, so it is always good to see something come together.

www.PacktPub.com

Support files, eBooks, discount offers, and more

For support files and downloads related to your book, please visit www.PacktPub.com.

Did you know that Packt offers eBook versions of every book published, with PDF and ePub files available? You can upgrade to the eBook version at www.PacktPub.com and as a print book customer, you are entitled to a discount on the eBook copy. Get in touch with us at service@packtpub.com for more details.

At www.PacktPub.com, you can also read a collection of free technical articles, sign up for a range of free newsletters and receive exclusive discounts and offers on Packt books and eBooks.

https://www2.packtpub.com/books/subscription/packtlib

Do you need instant solutions to your IT questions? PacktLib is Packt's online digital book library. Here, you can search, access, and read Packt's entire library of books.

Why subscribe?

- Fully searchable across every book published by Packt
- Copy and paste, print, and bookmark content
- On demand and accessible via a web browser

Free access for Packt account holders

If you have an account with Packt at www.PacktPub.com, you can use this to access PacktLib today and view 9 entirely free books. Simply use your login credentials for immediate access.

Table of Contents

Preface

Cocos2d is a cross-platform game engine for iOS and Android devices. Coding in Objective-C and using the rich graphical editor, you can push your game to both iOS and Android devices without any extra work. Cocos2d is packed with features that make game development simple, including integrated physics, particle engines, and a graphical editor for laying out your scenes and designing animations. Game development is about working out how to solve unique problems using the tools in your *development toolbox*. This book will help you to build this tool box, cover essential skills, and provide a solid foundation on which to grow your game development talent.

This book will introduce and develop your understanding of the core concepts and tools involved in developing games using Cocos2d, including the graphical development environment, SpriteBuilder, the built-in physics engine, the skills to show smooth-flowing animations, and techniques to develop easy to use and functional user interfaces.

Each chapter will introduce you to a new core skill. To practice this skill, in each chapter, you will develop a mini game that runs on both Android and iOS devices. Your skillset will evolve as you move through each chapter, and develop increasingly complex games.

What this book covers

Chapter 1, *Getting Started with Cocos2d*, discusses how to build your first cross-platform app using Cocos2d. We will install Cocos2d and get you all set up to create Cocos2d games. We will then walk through the template code and look at how it works.

Chapter 2, *Nodes, Sprites, and Scenes*, discusses the fundamental knowledge required to build any Cocos2d app. You will learn how to display a variety of content on the screen and transition between scenes. Here, you will discover how to lay the foundations of your game.

Chapter 3, *SpriteBuilder*, discusses how to create apps using the graphical Cocos2d editor. We will lay out scenes and build animations in the graphical editor.

Chapter 4, *Animation with SpriteBuilder*, covers a comprehensive overview of animations and actions and how to create them in code. We will also look at how to ease the animations to create an attractive and professional look.

Chapter 5, *User Interaction and Interface*, discusses, and, takes a look at, how to accept input from the user in a variety of ways. We will look at touches and gestures, accelerometer and interface controls.

Chapter 6, *Physics Engines*, discusses the location where we combine all our knowledge so far, with working physics to create fun physics-based apps. We will look at some basic physics concepts such as forces and joints, and then put it altogether in a scene and see what effects physics have on an app.

What you need for this book

In order to create games in Cocos2D-Swift, you will need a Mac computer with Xcode installed. If you want to put apps on an iOS device, you will need a paid iOS developer account from Apple. To put apps on an Android device, you will need an Android device running (at least Android 4.0 or a paid Apportable account) that allows apps to be built for Android 2.0+.

Who this book is for

This book is for developers with experience in Objective-C and iOS development who are looking to create a game for iOS or Android in Objective-C. It assumes that you understand the basic concepts of game development and just need an understanding of the framework. It covers the essential topics on how to create a game with Cocos2d v3. This would be a good book for someone with previous experience in Cocos2d and wants to learn about the changes in v3.

Conventions

In this book, you will find a number of styles of text that distinguish between different kinds of information. Here are some examples of these styles, and an explanation of their meaning.

Code words in text are shown as follows: "The `contentSize` property is the bounding box of the node."

A block of code is set as follows:

```
// Apple recommend assigning self with supers return value
  self = [super init];
  if (!self) return(nil);
```

New terms and **important words** are shown in bold. Words that you see on the screen, in menus or dialog boxes for example, appear in the text like this: "Press the **Publish** button. Your app will now be published on Xcode".

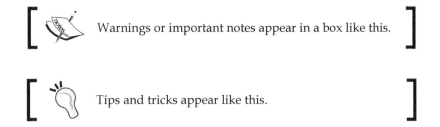

Warnings or important notes appear in a box like this.

Tips and tricks appear like this.

Reader feedback

Feedback from our readers is always welcome. Let us know what you think about this book — what you liked or may have disliked. Reader feedback is important for us to develop titles that you really get the most out of.

To send us general feedback, simply send an e-mail to feedback@packtpub.com, and mention the book title through the subject of your message.

If there is a topic that you have expertise in and you are interested in either writing or contributing to a book, see our author guide on www.packtpub.com/authors.

Customer support

Now that you are the proud owner of a Packt book, we have a number of things to help you to get the most from your purchase.

Downloading the example code

You can download the example code files for all Packt books you have purchased from your account at http://www.packtpub.com. If you purchased this book elsewhere, you can visit http://www.packtpub.com/support and register to have the files e-mailed directly to you.

Downloading the color images of this book

We also provide you with a PDF file that has color images of the screenshots / diagrams used in this book. The color images will help you better understand the changes in the output. You can download this file from: https://www.packtpub.com/sites/default/files/downloads/B03446_ColoredImages.pdf

Errata

Although we have taken every care to ensure the accuracy of our content, mistakes do happen. If you find a mistake in one of our books—maybe a mistake in the text or the code—we would be grateful if you would report this to us. By doing so, you can save other readers from frustration and help us improve subsequent versions of this book. If you find any errata, please report them by visiting http://www.packtpub.com/support, selecting your book, clicking on the **errata submission form** link, and entering the details of your errata. Once your errata are verified, your submission will be accepted and the errata will be uploaded to our website, or added to any list of existing errata, under the Errata section of that title.

Piracy

Piracy of copyright material on the Internet is an ongoing problem across all media. At Packt, we take the protection of our copyright and licenses very seriously. If you come across any illegal copies of our works, in any form, on the Internet, please provide us with the location address or website name immediately so that we can pursue a remedy.

Please contact us at copyright@packtpub.com with a link to the suspected pirated material.

We appreciate your help in protecting our authors, and our ability to bring you valuable content.

Questions

You can contact us at questions@packtpub.com if you are having a problem with any aspect of the book, and we will do our best to address it.

1
Getting Started with Cocos2d

In this chapter, you will learn how to create your first Cocos2d project. You will make a simple game that could be extended to a full title if you choose. You will also learn how to deploy on Android using Apportable.

In this Chapter, we will cover the following topics:

- Installing Cocos2d
- Working of the Cocos2d app
- Creating a project with the template

An introduction to Cocos2d

Cocos2d for iPhone is an open source framework to build cross-platform 2D games with **Xcode** and **Objective-C**. Cocos2d is licensed by Massachusetts Institute of Technology (MIT), meaning that in addition to being free to use, there is no need to open source your game, and no licensing or profit share fees to pay to use it in a commercial product.

Cocos2d can be compiled for iOS and Android using the tool **Apportable**, the official sponsor of the Cocos2d project. This framework encourages and allows you to be creative; its visual editor, **SpriteBuilder**, allows you to create and lay out scenes, design animations, and play around with physics and sprite sheets. Cocos2d is built on top of OpenGL ES 2.0, and the layer between the two has been highly optimized over a period of time. It also supports custom OpenGL shaders when you want to change the way your scene is rendered by OpenGL.

You might be wondering why you should use Cocos2d in the newly released Apple native library, SpriteKit, and I believe the answer is relatively simple. Cocos2d is a far more mature library than SpriteKit, and it has more features while still being easier to use. Cocos2d is also open source, which means you can add to it if needed, and see how it works behind the scenes. However, the real advantage of Cocos2d over SpriteKit is its cross-platform ability; Cocos2d can be cross-compiled to Android from Objective-C. This might sound like magic; I wouldn't be surprised if a bit of magic was involved, but it does work, and you will see it work in this book. Cocos2d is also fully compatible with Swift, Apple's new programming language, which was unveiled in June 2014. While Swift has created a considerable buzz, Objective-C will nevertheless be essential for anyone wishing to work with Cocos2d. If you are using Objective-C, another benefit is that Cocos2d supports iOS5+ unlike SpriteKit, which only supports iOS 7+.

Installing Cocos2d

Before you can do anything, you need to install Cocos2d. Let's get started.

There are several ways to install Cocos2d. Some methods are easy, whereas some are harder to get started, but it will make upgrading in the future much easier. Before you install Cocos2d, you need to ensure that you have the latest version of Xcode installed. Xcode can be found on the Mac App Store or on the Apple Developer Program portal. Additionally, to push your apps into an iOS device, you will need a paid iOS developers account. New accounts can be made at `http://developer.apple.com/ios`.

Installing Cocos2d with the installer

Using the installer is the easiest method of installation and is recommended for first time users because it will install the relevant documentation and project templates automatically.

To install Cocos2d with the installer, follow these steps:

1. Download the latest version of the installer from `http://www.cocos2d-swift.org/download`

2. Open the installer and follow the prompts to install Cocos2d.

3. Go to the Mac App Store and install **SpriteBuilder**; we will use this in later chapters.

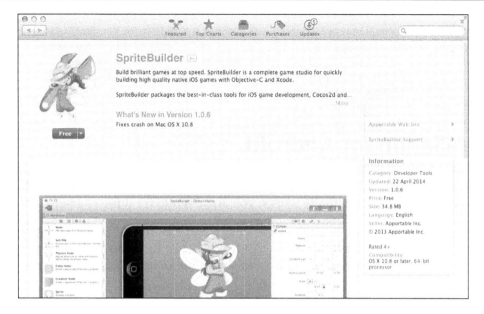

Creating a Hello World project

You can start by creating a new project from the template that you just installed in Xcode. Open up Xcode and click **New Project**. You will see a new section in the templates for **cocos2d v3.x**. Click on this, and create a new project with the **cocos2d iOS** template, as shown in the following figure. You can now build and run the template, and have a play around with the example app:

Cocos2D-Swift Version 3 was a minor upgrade from Version 2. Its main features were an official support for Android, built-in physics engine, and a cleaned up API. As part of the API cleanup, many classes were either renamed or removed all together. This can make it difficult to follow tutorials from old versions.

Installation for Android

To build and run the Cocos2d app for Android, you need to install Apportable, a cross-compiler that will compile the Objective-C code to run on Android devices. This sounds crazy, but it actually works; you are about to try it for yourself.

You will also need to plug in an Android device and ensure that USB debugging is enabled. This step is different for every Android device, so if you are not sure how to do it, the best method is to go online and search for `Enable USB debugging on <device name>`.

The first step is to download and install Apportable, the instructions for which can be found at `https://www.Apportable.com`. You will be asked to sign up to an account, but it is completely free to build Cocos2d games; you can even push your game to the Google Play Store. The steps on how to install your app in your Android phone are as follows:

1. Once you have installed Apportable, open a terminal window and navigate to the Hello World project folder.

2. From inside the project folder, run the command `Apportable load`.

3. You will then be asked a series of questions. First, you will be asked whether your app is using OpenGL ES 1 or 2. Answer with 2. The difference between these options is that Cocos2d v3 is built on top of Open GL ES v2. They have a different API and so selecting the correct option is important.

4. The next question will ask whether your app should initially launch in portrait or landscape. Obviously, this will change between projects, but for now, answer **L** for landscape.

5. You will then see a large amount of terminal output while Apportable builds the project. Once the build is complete, Apportable will attempt to install your app in the Android device that is plugged into your computer.

Once the app is installed, it will automatically open. If your phone is locked, you will have to manually unlock it.

Template project code breakdown

Now that you have successfully built and deployed your first Cocos2d app, let's see how it actually works. In Xcode, open up `IntroScene.m`.

IntroScene.m

The IntroScene.m file corresponds with the first scene you see when you load up your app. We will go into more detail on scenes in the next chapter, but for now, all you need to know is what a scene looks like. The first part of the init() method is a slightly different method compared to the standard Objective-C init pattern.

1. First, assign `self`, and then check to make sure that it did not return `nil`. This is a standard Objective-C pattern to guard against a sub-class or super class not initiating properly:

    ```
    // Apple recommend assigning self with supers return value
        self = [super init];
        if (!self) return(nil);
    ```

2. Next, is your first piece of Cocos2d code:

    ```
    // Create a colored background (Dark Grey)
        CCNodeColor *background = [CCNodeColor nodeWithColor:[CCColor
    colorWithRed:0.2f green:0.2f blue:0.2f alpha:1.0f]];
        [self addChild:background];
    ```

    `CCNodeColor` is a Cocos2d object that allows you to create and display a rectangle of a single color.

3. You create the color node by passing in the color that you want in Cocos2d; colors are represented by the `CCColor` class. For now, you are making a dark gray background, but experiment by changing the color values, and then building and running the app to see the effect.

4. Once you have created the color node, you need to add it to the scene so that Cocos2d knows how to render it. Until you add it, it will not be visible on screen. You add the background child to self, which in this case is the intro scene.

5. Now, you have a solid background color, but the app is still pretty boring. Let's add some text to say 'Hello World':

    ```
    // Hello World
        CCLabelTTF *label = [CCLabelTTF labelWithString:@"Hello World"
    fontName:@"Chalkduster" fontSize:36.0f];
    ```

```
label.positionType = CCPositionTypeNormalized;
label.color = [CCColor redColor];
label.position = ccp(0.5f, 0.5f); // Middle of screen
[self addChild:label];
```

CCLabelTTF is a label class that allows you to add text to your scene. Labels are created by passing in a string, a font name, and a font size, and then setting a position type. Position types will be covered in the next chapter as well, but a normalized position type allows you to position your node with a percentage from the left and bottom, rather than a fixed position. This is of great value when you are developing an app that will run on multiple screen sizes, such as Android phones and tablets. Set the label color to red and then set the position to (0.5, 0.5) using ccp, which is Cocos2d shorthand for making a new CGPoint array. Points in Cocos2d have an origin at the bottom-left of the scene. Remember that this is a percentage, so we are placing it 50 percent in and 50 percent up, which is the center of the screen. Once you have finished setting up your label, you add it to the scene so that it will be rendered.

Now you need a way to get to the next scene, where your game will have some interaction. You need to add a button:

```
// Helloworld scene button
CCButton *helloWorldButton = [CCButton buttonWithTitle:@"[ Start
]" fontName:@"Verdana-Bold" fontSize:18.0f];
    helloWorldButton.positionType = CCPositionTypeNormalized;
    helloWorldButton.position = ccp(0.5f, 0.35f);
    [helloWorldButton setTarget:self selector:@
selector(onSpinningClicked:)];
    [self addChild:helloWorldButton];
```

CCButton is a button node that gives you a target and a selector for when the node is tapped on. You can also set a block to run on tap instead, but in this example, we are using the target / selector paradigm. You create the button in a similar way to the label with a string, font name, font size, and position. The difference now is that you also need to set the target and selector. You will need to set the target to self, and run a method that is in this class, which for this example is onSpinningClicked. Add this button to the scene to be rendered as well.

Let's have a look at the method that is called when you tap the button:

```
- (void)onSpinningClicked:(id)sender
{
    // start spinning scene with transition
    [[CCDirector sharedDirector] replaceScene:[HelloWorldScene scene]
                            withTransition:[CCTransition transition
PushWithDirection:CCTransitionDirectionLeft duration:1.0f]];
}
```

In this method, you are making a call to the `CCDirector`: the director of the game that manages the scene currently on the screen to replace the current scene with the `HelloWorld` scene. We will use a transition to do this, which will be covered fully later in this book. For now, we will start with a simple transition that will push the new scene that comes in from the left. You don't have to use a transition, but can add a nice bit of polish to your game.

The HelloWorldScene.m class

Let's take a look at the scene you have transitioned to. If you play around with the app you will see that you have an image that is rotating, and that starts in the center of the screen. When you tap the screen, it moves to where you tapped. Let's see how this works.

1. Starting in the `init` method, the first part is always the same, but there is something new now:

    ```
    // Apple recommend assigning self with supers return value
    self = [super init];
    if (!self) return(nil);
    // Enable touch handling on scene node
    self.userInteractionEnabled = YES;
    ```

    Enabled user interaction tells the `CCDirector` class that you want the scene to receive touches. This is so that when you tap the screen, your image moves.

2. Next, you create the background in the same way as in `IntroScene.m`. The following code is another new concept:

    ```
    // Add a sprite
    _sprite = [CCSprite spriteWithImageNamed:@"Icon-72.png"];
    _sprite.position  = ccp(self.contentSize.width/2,self.
    contentSize.height/2);
    [self addChild:_sprite];
    ```

    You are now creating the image that starts in the middle of the screen. These images are known as **sprites**, and they are created using their image names. Using the names makes Cocos2d look for an image in the app bundle, with the name you provide. You save the sprite reference in an instance variable, so it can be moved around the screen. Then, the position of the sprite is set to start in the center of the screen. Note that this is different to the position type that was used before; now you are setting it to a fixed coordinate rather than a percentage. Then, add the sprite to the scene to be rendered.

The Cocos2d template stores its nodes in instance variables. Apple recommends against this practice, stating that the preferred method to store variables accessible within a class is through properties. Apple's recommended practice will be used in this book. More information can be found at https://developer.apple. com/library/mac/documentation/Cocoa/Conceptual/ ProgrammingWithObjectiveC/EncapsulatingData/ EncapsulatingData.html.

3. Now, you will add an animation to your sprite in order to make it spin:

```
// Animate sprite with action
CCActionRotateBy* actionSpin = [CCActionRotateBy
actionWithDuration:1.5f angle:360];
    [_sprite runAction:[CCActionRepeatForever
actionWithAction:actionSpin]];
```

This code creates a CCActionRotateBy action with a duration of 1.5 seconds and an angle of 360 degrees clockwise. This means that you want the sprite to rotate once by 360 degrees, and take 1.5 seconds to complete the rotation. You will notice that in the app, the rotation runs continuously; this is achieved on the next line with the relatively self-explanatory CCActionRepeatForever action. You then run the action on your sprite in order to start the rotation. There are many different types of CCAction that will be covered in this book; we have only just touched the surface of what is possible with this example:

```
// Create a back button
    CCButton *backButton = [CCButton buttonWithTitle:@"[ Menu ]"
fontName:@"Verdana-Bold" fontSize:18.0f];
    backButton.positionType = CCPositionTypeNormalized;
    backButton.position = ccp(0.85f, 0.95f); // Top Right of
screen
    [backButton setTarget:self selector:@
selector(onBackClicked:)];
    [self addChild:bcackButton];
```

4. Next, you create a button that will take you back to the main menu. This works exactly the same as in the previous scene.

5. Now, let's look at how you handle touch. Scroll down to the code and find the `touchBegan` method.

 In Xcode, you can use Ctrl+6 and start typing the method you are looking for. This is a quick way to navigate code.

```
-(void) touchBegan:(UITouch *)touch withEvent:(UIEvent *)event {
    CGPoint touchLoc = [touch locationInNode:self];

    // Log touch location
    CCLOG(@"Move sprite to @ %@",NSStringFromCGPoint(touchLoc));

    // Move our sprite to touch location
    CCActionMoveTo *actionMove = [CCActionMoveTo
actionWithDuration:1.0f position:touchLoc];
    [_sprite runAction:actionMove];
}
```

How does `touchBegan` work? It gets activated when you first touch the screen, and you get a location of touch translated into the coordinate space of your node. This is an important step because **UIKit** (the framework used by iOS) uses a different coordinate space to Cocos2d and OpenGL. If the location doesn't get translated, you would end up moving your node to the wrong position on the screen.

 It is important to note the difference between `touchBegan` and `touchEnded`. Choosing the correct one depends on what you are trying to achieve with your UI. If you want an action to occur as soon as the user touches the screen, then use `touchBegan`. If you want an action to occur when the user lifts their finger, then use `touchEnded`.

The template then logs the position that you are moving the sprite to, using a `CCLog` – a macro helper that allows you to disable logging in release builds.

Next, you will create a `CCActionMoveTo` action. This action is similar to `CCActionRotateBy`, but now you are moving a node to an identified position rather than rotating a node by an angle. You want your sprite to move to the touch position, using the touch location that was translated. For this example, you want the move to take 1 second, but feel free to change the duration and rebuild to see the effects. Once you have created the action, run it on the sprite. Note that you are using the instance variable that was created in the `init` method.

Summary

Congratulations! You have built your first cross-platform app and stepped through the code to see how it works. At this point, you should have a basic idea of how a Cocos2d app is put together. You have created scenes to contain different screens of your game, and you have used the CCDirector class to move between them. You have created different types of nodes to display content on the screen, including CCLabelTTF for text content, CCButton to create a button on screen, and CCSprite to display an image. You have used CCActions in the form of CCActionRotateBy and CCActionMoveTo, and you modified their behavior using CCActionRepeatForever. You also learned how to create a solid rectangle of color using CCNodeColor.

You should now have a play with the sample code and see what you can do. Try changing the durations and text, and the colors of the background. You could also try to replace the image with your own or have more than one image.

In the next chapter, you will build on the knowledge gained in this chapter by going over the details of nodes, sprites and scenes. You will also build your very first game and deploy it to your device.

2
Nodes, Sprites, and Scenes

In the last chapter, you went through the introduction of Cocos2d template. You had a look at your first nodes, and sprites, and learned how to move between scenes. In this chapter, you will get into more detail on how these elements work and what can be done with them. You will also create your first mini game to begin with, to see how the pieces all come together.

In this chapter, you will learn:

- How to build blocks of Cocos2d nodes
- How to display images on the screen
- How to layout your scene
- How to change between different scenes

The building blocks, nodes

In Cocos2d, everything you see on screen is a subclass of the CCNode class. Even the scenes your game has are subclasses of the CCNode class.

There are some important subclasses that will be used in almost every game. Therefore, it is important to know them. These are as follows:

- CCSprite: This represents an image that can be animated
- CCNodeColor: This is a plain colored node
- CCLabelTTF: This is a node that renders text in any TrueType font
- CCButton: This is an interactive node that can have an action attached
- CCLayoutBox: This is a node that lays out other nodes in a vertical or horizontal layout

[💡 The CCLayoutBox node replaces the CCMenu class, which was in the previous versions of Cocos2d.]

The reason every class inherits from the CCNode class is that there are some important properties that all visible elements on-screen need. These are as follows:

- contentSize: This is the size of the element in the unit that is specified in the contentSizeType property
- position: This is the position (*x, y*) of the node in the unit that is specified in the positionType property
- anchorPoint: This is the center point for rotation and the reference point to position the node
- visible: This defines whether the node is visible or not

The following screenshot illustrates these properties:

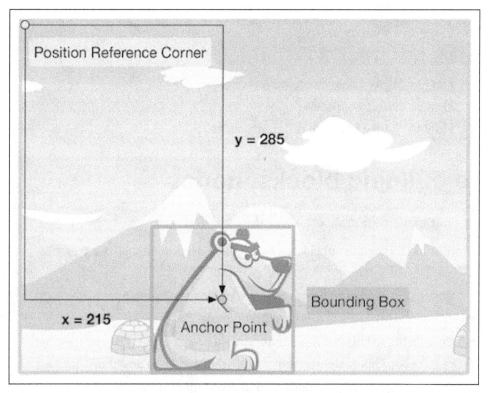

Source: https://www.makegameswith.us/docs/#!/cocos2d/1.0/nodes

There are two properties that can affect where each node is positioned on the screen. These are the `Position Reference Corner` and the `Anchor Point` properties. By default, the reference corner is at the bottom-left corner. This can be changed to any corner and in the image shown, it is set to be at the top-left. This can be helpful when working with other coordinate systems that use a different zero position such as **UIKit**.

The anchor point of the node defaults to (`0.5, 0.5`). Anchor points are the (*x, y*) point between `0` and `1`. `0` means the left-bottom edge and 1 is the top-right edge. The (`0.5, 0.5`) values places the anchor point at the direct center of the image. The anchor point is also used as the center of rotation, as seen in the following screenshot:

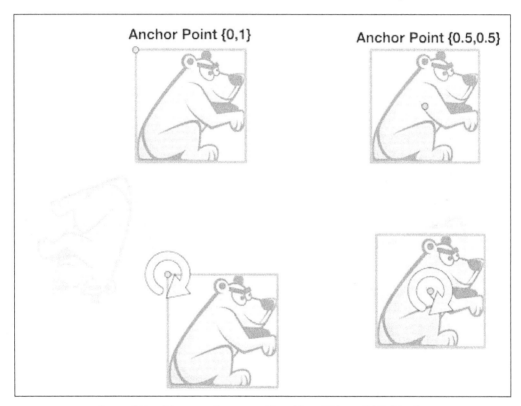

Source: https://www.makegameswith.us/docs/#!/cocos2d/1.0/nodes

The `contentSize` property is the bounding box of the node. This might not seem to be important, but it actually has a great effect on the node. Remember that our anchor points are expressed as a normalized point, and as such the bounding box needs to be correct. When using a sprite, the bounding box is set to be the size of the image.

The position of the node is always specified relative to its parent node, by default the relative is positioned at the bottom-left corner of the parent. Cocos2d however supports multiple sizing and position types that can be used to layout your scene.

There are three position types to choose from based on your needs:

1. **Points**: This is the default option. Points are scaled by the `UIScaleFactor` property. This is used to move between different screen sizes such as phone to tablet. It is generally not flexible enough to handle all the screen sizes of Android.
2. **UI Points**: This option does not get scaled. A position with this type will always be exactly on-screen as it has been set.
3. **Normalized**: This position is expressed from zero to one. It is relative to the size of the parent, and can be very useful to center a node on the screen. It is also quite helpful to deal with multiple screen sizes.

There are five content size types to choose from. These can be set individually for the width and height. These are as follows:

1. **Points**: This is the default option. As is the case with position, it is scaled based on the `UIScaleFactor` property.
2. **UI Points**: This size is specified based on exact points. It is not scaled.
3. **Normalized**: This size is expressed relative to its parent from 0 to 1.
4. **Inset points**: This node will be the size of the parents minus the inset points defined. This type is scaled based on the `UIScaleFactor` property.
5. **Inset UI points**: This is similar to the preceding point, but not scaled.

There is a huge list of options, but it is handy to know what is available. Most of the time you will use the scaling options for background nodes, and the fixed options for foreground nodes such as characters and sprites.

Children nodes

Nodes can also have children. You can add any node as a child of any other node. This is how a node hierarchy is formed. The base node of every scene is indeed the `CCScene` class itself.

Adding children

To add a node as a child, use the following method:

```
[parent addChild:childNode];
```

Objects are displayed in the order they were added to the node. The first added is at the bottom and everything after that is added at the top. This is especially important when you have overlapping children as it will determine what you see on-screen. This order can be changed, and is covered later in the chapter.

The position of the node is always relative to the parent. The only exception to this rule is with nodes that have a physics body. This will be covered in *Chapter 6, Physics Engines*. All the children of a node are moved together with the parent node. This is a very useful and important concept to grasp. Imagine a complex character on-screen. The character is made up of many sprites. There is one for the head, two for the arms, one for the body, and so on. Now, you want to move the character to the other side of the screen. You could do it as follows:

```
head.position = ccp(250, 250);
arm1.position = ccp(250, 250);
arm2.position = ccp(250, 250);
body.position = ccp(250, 250);
```

Even this wouldn't work because you would then have to offset each body part, so they aren't just sitting on top of each other. Instead, what you should do is make one CCNode instance for our character and add every other node to it:

```
CCNode *character = [CCNode node];

//Setup our sprites with normalized positions
head.position = ccp(0.5, 0.1);
arm1.position = ccp(0.25, 0.25);
arm2.position = ccp(0.75, 0.25);
body.position = ccp(0.5, 0.5);

//Add them as children to our character CCNode
[character addChild:head];
[character addChild:arm1];
[character addChild:arm2];
[character addChild:body];

//Remember to set the content size and add it to the scene
[self addChild:character];
character.contentSize = CGRectMake(100, 300);
```

It is more work to set up, but you will probably want to move your character around quite a lot in your game. Now, when you want to set the position of the character, you simply move that node:

```
character.position = ccp(250, 250);
```

All our children will move with the node and remain positioned correctly with each other.

Removing children

To remove a child from a node, you can simply call:

```
[node removeChild:childToRemove];
```

However, sometimes it is easier to call through:

```
[childToRemove removeFromParent];
```

The choice is up to you as a developer.

Drawing order of the children nodes

The drawing order of children is defined by the zOrder property of each node. The zOrder property is simply a number that tells Cocos2d the order in which the nodes will be drawn on screen.

By default, children are drawn on top of their parents. You can think of zOrder as the depth on screen to place the objects. It determines the nodes' position in the stack of objects to be drawn. You can modify this behavior by setting a custom zOrder. This can be done at the time the child is added to the parent:

```
[parent addChild:child z:5]
```

You can also set the zOrder property of a node. The zOrder property changes the position of the node in the draw order. The first node added is drawn first, and then the second node is drawn on top of this, and so on. This is also how objects with the same zOrder are drawn. Whoever had the zOrder first is drawn first.

The drawing order is defined as follows:

1. Draw all children with a zOrder less than zero. The lowest value is drawn first.
2. Draw self.
3. Draw all children with a zOrder greater-than or equal to zero. Nodes that were added first are drawn first.

If you want a node to appear below its parent, set its zOrder property to a negative number:

```
node.zOrder = -1;
```

Working with multiple coordinate systems

By default, node positions are expressed relative to their parent. It can be useful to break out of the parent's coordinate system, and calculate the position in the world. This could be used with our character to see whether its arm has exited the screen.

To calculate the position of a node in world space, the following method is used:

```
CGPoint worldPosition = [parentNode convertToWorldSpace:childNode.
position];
```

This gives the world coordinate of the child node. If it is then required to calculate the position of the child node that is relative to another node, the following method can be used:

```
CGPoint scenePosition = [scene convertToNodeSpace:worldPosition];
```

We now have our child node's position relative to our scene. Now, instead of converting from the node space of your scene, you can convert to the node space of any node.

Sprites

Sprites in Cocos2d are represented by the CCSprite class. A sprite is any 2D image. You can create a sprite with an image from the bundle or a subrectangle of another image.

Sprites are created from bundle images as follows:

```
CCSprite sprite = [CCSprite spriteWithImageNamed:@"myImage.png"];
```

This will create a sprite object. Remember you still need to set its position, and then add it to the scene before it's rendered.

Putting it into practice

It's now time to start working on your first game. You will put all the information you have learned so far into practice, and create a very simple game using nodes and sprites. The game will be a simple one where you try to catch water in a bucket. The game will get faster and faster as it goes on. It's probably not going to make you the next App Store millionaire, but you have to start somewhere right?

Here is what our game will look like when it is finished:

Start by making a new Cocos2d project in Xcode just like you did in the last chapter. You can also delete the `HelloWorldScene` classes as you won't be using them.

Open up the `IntroScene.m` file, and delete all the code from the `init` method, except the required initialization and return statement. Also, you can delete the `onSpinningClicked` method. You should end up with an implementation, as shown in the following code:

```
@implementation IntroScene

// --------------------------------------------------------------------
-----
#pragma mark - Create & Destroy
// --------------------------------------------------------------------
-----

+ (IntroScene *)scene
{
    return [[self alloc] init];
}
```

```
// --------------------------------------------------------------------
-----

- (id)init
{
    // Apple recommend assigning self with supers return value
    self = [super init];
    if (!self) return(nil);

    return self;
}

@end
```

Download the assets from `https://s3.amazonaws.com/mgwu-misc/Spritebuilder+Tutorial/PeevedPenguinsAssets.zip`. Unzip the assets and add them to the project.

First, you will need to add some properties so that you can keep a reference to our game items. Add a private interface at the top of your `IntroScene.m` file:

```
@interface IntroScene()

@property (nonatomic) CCNode *waterBucket;
@property (nonatomic) CCLabelTTF *scoreLabel;
@property (nonatomic) NSMutableArray *drops;
@property (nonatomic, assign) int bucketPosition;
@property (nonatomic, assign) int numberDropped;
@end
```

You will also need to define how many places you want water drops to fall from. Add a constant just below the interface:

```
static const int kNumberOfPositions = 4;
```

These properties will be used so that you can reference your game items in all the methods in your game. You will create them in the `init` method and then move them in the `Touch` event method. Therefore, you will need a property so that you can access them.

Adding nodes to the scene

Let's get started, go to the `init` method and add the following code:

```
    self.userInteractionEnabled = YES;
    CCPositionType positionType = CCPositionTypeMake
(CCPositionUnitNormalized, CCPositionUnitNormalized,
CCPositionReferenceCornerBottomLeft);
```

You will be using normalized coordinates to lay out your scene. This will make the game resize better when ported to Android devices.

Now, let's create sprites for use in the game. The designer provided two images for the water bucket: a top part and a bottom part. This is because we can make the water drop seem like it is falling into the bucket rather than behind the bucket. In this quick example, it will be kept simple by just making it fall behind, but as an extension you should try to make the water drop fall into the bucket. Add the following code to the `init` method:

```
//Create the water bucket
    CCNode *waterBucket = [CCNode node];
    CCSprite *bucketBottom = [CCSprite spriteWithImageNamed:@"bucket_
bottom.png"];
    CCSprite *bucketTop = [CCSprite spriteWithImageNamed:@"bucket_top.
png"];
```

First, you create a node to keep your sprites in, and then load up the images from the bundle. Now, let's position them and add them to the `waterBucket` node. Add the following code:

```
bucketBottom.positionType = positionType;
    bucketTop.positionType = positionType;

    bucketBottom.anchorPoint = ccp(0.5, 0.0);
    bucketBottom.position = ccp(0.5, 0.0);

    bucketTop.anchorPoint = ccp(0.5, 1.0);
    bucketTop.position = ccp(0.5, 1.0);

    [waterBucket addChild:bucketTop];
    [waterBucket addChild:bucketBottom];
```

The code pins the bottom bucket to the bottom of the node, and the top sprite to the top of the node. Next, you need to configure your `waterBucket` node. Add the following code:

```
waterBucket.contentSize = CGSizeMake(bucketBottom.contentSize.width,
bucketBottom.contentSize.height + bucketTop.contentSize.height);
    waterBucket.positionType = positionType;
    waterBucket.anchorPoint = ccp(0.5, 0.5);
    waterBucket.position = ccp(0.5, 0.15);
    [self addChild:waterBucket z:1];
    self.waterBucket = waterBucket;
```

Notice that the water bucket has a `zOrder` of one. This is because it will appear above any water drops that are later added to the scene.

It is a good practice to create a method to handle in order to set up a new game. This allows you to easily restart your game. Add the following `newGame` method to the class.

```
- (void)newGame {
    //Reset the properties
    self.numberDropped = 0;
    self.bucketPosition = 0;
    //If we already have drops, remove them from the parent
    if (self.drops) {
        for (CCNode *drop in self.drops) {
            [drop removeFromParent];
        }
    }
    //Setup a new drops array
    self.drops = [NSMutableArray array];

    //Reset the score label
    self.scoreLabel.string = @"Score: 0";
}
```

Go back and add a call method to your new game method at the end of the `init` method, right before the return method.

Build and run your code to see your progress. You should see a water bucket on the screen sitting at the left-hand side:

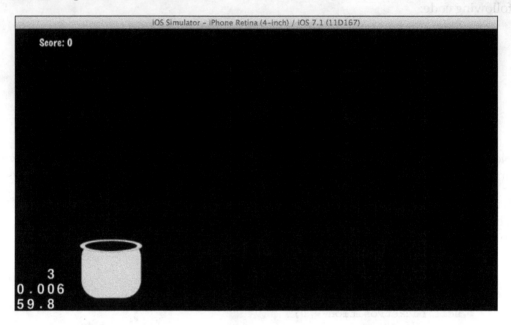

There will also be a score label up at the top. Looks like a pretty boring game so far. So, let's add some interactivity.

Detecting touches and responding

We will now add the Touch methods so that your game has some interactivity

Add the following code to the class:

```
#pragma mark - Touch Methods

- (void)touchBegan:(UITouch *)touch withEvent:(UIEvent *)event {
    CGPoint touchLocation = [touch locationInNode:self];
    CGFloat halfWay = self.contentSize.width/2;

    if (touchLocation.x < halfWay) {
        self.bucketPosition--;
    } else {
        self.bucketPosition++;
    }
}
```

```
}

#pragma mark - Custom Setters/Getters

- (void)setBucketPosition:(int)bucketPosition {
    //Limit the values of this property
    if (bucketPosition < 0) {
        bucketPosition = 0;
    } else if (bucketPosition > kNumberOfPositions-1) {
        bucketPosition = kNumberOfPositions - 1;
    }

    //Update the position of the water bucket
    _bucketPosition = bucketPosition;
    CGFloat positionX = (float)(1 + bucketPosition) / ((float)
kNumberOfPositions+1);

    self.waterBucket.position = ccp(positionX, self.waterBucket.
position.y);
}
```

The first method handles the bucket position when the user touches down on the screen. The way it will work is when the user touches the left-hand side of the screen, you move the bucket to the left. When you touch the right-hand side of the screen, the bucket will move to the right. The code is using the `contentSize` property of the scene to calculate where the halfway point is. It then sets the `bucketPosition` property.

The next method is a custom setter for the property. The first part limits the range of the property between zero and the constant that was defined at the top of the class. Once the new value has been calculated, you store the value and calculate the new position of the bucket sprite. You can then set the position of the bucket.

 It is always a good idea to use pragma marks to separate the sections of your class. It helps to keep it organized and is also used by Xcode to search and navigate your code.

Build and run the game now, and you should be able to move the bucket left and right.

Now that you can move the bucket around, it would be a bit more interesting to see whether there was something to catch. The game needs a method to create the water drops. Add the following method:

```
- (void) spawnWaterDrop {
    CCPositionType positionType = CCPositionTypeMake
(CCPositionUnitNormalized, CCPositionUnitNormalized,
CCPositionReferenceCornerBottomLeft);
    CGFloat positionX = (1 + (float)arc4random_
uniform(kNumberOfPositions)) / ((float)kNumberOfPositions + 1);
    CCSprite *waterDrop = [CCSprite spriteWithImageNamed:@"water_drop.
png"];
    waterDrop.positionType = positionType;
    waterDrop.anchorPoint = ccp(0.5, 0.0);
    waterDrop.position = ccp(positionX, 1.0);
    [self addChild:waterDrop];
    CGFloat time = 3.0 - (self.numberDropped / 10.0);
    CCActionMoveTo *move = [CCActionMoveTo actionWithDuration:time
position:ccp(positionX, 0)];
    [waterDrop runAction:move];
    [self.drops addObject:waterDrop];
    self.numberDropped++;
}
```

This method creates a new water drop, positions it, and adds it to the view hierarchy. Notice that it uses a `CCActionMoveTo` class reference to move the sprite down the screen. We use an equation to speed up the water drops based on the number that were caught:

```
CGFloat time = 3.0 - (self.numberDropped / 10.0);
```

Another new concept is the `arc4random_uniform(x)` function. This method creates a random number between *0* and less-than *x*. It is always an integer; so if you need a random decimal number, you need to divide after generating the random integer:

```
CGFloat positionX = (1 + (float)arc4random_
uniform(kNumberOfPositions)) / ((float)kNumberOfPositions + 1);
```

Add a method call to the bottom of the `newGame` method to call the new `spawnWaterDrop` method:

```
[self spawnWaterDrop];
```

The game is almost complete; the only thing left to do is check whether the bucket is underneath each water drop when they reach the bottom. This will be accomplished using the Cocos2d `update` method. This method is called every time a frame is drawn to the screen. Using this is simple, it is just overridden on the `scene` class.

Add the following method to the class:

```
- (void)update:(CCTime)delta {
    //Check every drop on screen
    for (int i = self.drops.count-1; i>=0; i--) {
        CCNode *drop = self.drops[i];
        //First check if the water drop has reached the bucket height
        if (drop.position.y <= self.waterBucket.position.y) {
            //Water drop is at bucket height
            //Next check if the bucket is in the correct position
            if (drop.position.x == self.waterBucket.position.x) {

                //If it is remove the drop from the screen
                [drop removeFromParent];
                [self.drops removeObject:drop];

                //Update the score
                self.scoreLabel.string = [NSString
    stringWithFormat:@"Score: %d", self.numberDropped];

                //Create a new drop
                [self spawnWaterDrop];
            } else {
                //The drop was missed, start a new game
                [self newGame];
            }
        }
    }
}
```

Now in every frame, the water drops are checked to see whether they have reached the bottom of the screen. If they have, check to see whether the bucket is in the right position. If it is, we add 1 to the score. If it's not, the game is restarted.

The game is now complete.

Build and run the game now. It should be fully playable.

The next step

Congratulations on making your first game in Cocos2d. There are many possible extensions you could make:

1. The game currently only drops one drop at a time. It was set up to use an array for drops; however, you should be able to easily drop more than one drop at once.

2. Currently the drop falls behind the water bucket; this is not what the designer intended. Modify the game so the drop falls into the bucket, as shown in the following figure:

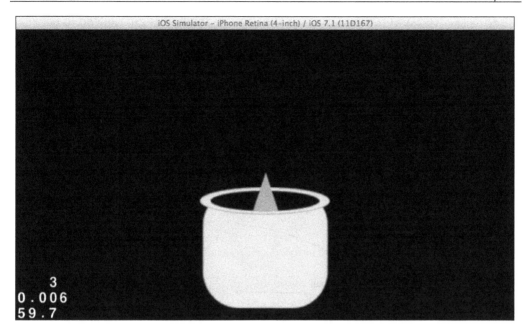

 Don't forget that you can always build and run your app for Android using Apportable.

The Cocos2d update loop

In our game, the update method was seen for the first time. This will most likely be used in every game, so it will now be covered in more detail.

There are two types of update methods:

- `update:(CCTime)delta`: This update method has a dynamic time step. It is called directly before the frame is rendered. Cocos2d attempts to render your game at 60 frames per second.

 If your game consumes too much processing time, then the game's frame rate will decrease. The update method will then be called less-than 60 times per second.

The `delta` parameter shows the time since the last `update` call in milliseconds.

- `fixedUpdate:(CCTime)delta`: This update method is guaranteed to be called at a specified interval. It is recommended to use this when you require property changes on physics-based objects. The integrated physics engine operates on this update method.

These update methods are available inside every `CCNode`. The update method is called on each node by the `CCDirector` class.

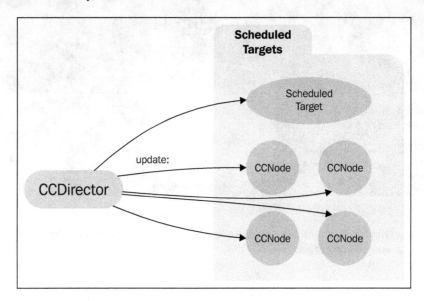

The `update` loop is often used as an alternative to the `CCAction` class as it allows much more flexibility. More of this will be covered in *Chapter 4*, *Animation with SpriteBuilder*. For example, you could move a character using the `update` loop as follows:

```
- (void)update:(CCTime)delta {
    // move character to the right, 100 points a second
    self.character.position = ccp(self.character.position.x +
100*delta, self.character.position.y);
}
```

Notice that the change in position is multiplied by the delta parameter. This will cause your character to move 100 points per second no matter what the frame rate is. Sometimes, it can be desirable, whereas at other times, it can be the wrong choice. This topic will be covered extensively in *Chapter 4*, *Animation with SpriteBuilder*.

Scenes

Scenes in Cocos2d are used extensively to break the game into manageable components. While it would be possible to create your entire game in one scene, it is certainly not advisable. The scene is the root node of your node hierarchy. Each scene is a subclass of the CCNode class. Only one scene can be active at any time, and changing the active scene is managed by the CCDirector class .

Scene life cycle

Cocos2d provides multiple events that are called at certain points in the life cycle of your scene. You can override these events in any CCNode subclass, and not just the CCScene class. The following events are available:

- init: This method is called when a scene is initialized in code. If the scene was created in SpriteBuilder, this method is not called. This method is normally where you build your scene by adding child nodes.

- didLoadFromCCB: This method is called when your scene is created in SpriteBuilder. It is called when the complete scene is loaded and all the code connections have been set up. You can implement this method to access and manipulate the content of the scene, often achieving results that are not possible inside SpriteBuilder. You cannot access the child nodes or code connections before this method is called.

- onEnter: This method is called as soon as the replacement of the current active scene begins. It is called before any animated transition occurs. This method is used to configure your scene before the scene can be seen on screen.

- onEnterTransitionDidFinish: If you are using an animated scene transition, this method is called on completion of the animation. If you are not using a transition, it is called right after the onEnter event. Implement this method to execute the code right after the transition is finished. This is often used to start off the scene's animations or interactivity.

- onExit: This method is called when the scene leaves the stage. If the scene is using an animated transition, then it is called when the transition has finished.

- onExitTransitionDidStart: This method is called when the scene begins to exit at the start of the transition.

You must call super when overriding the onEnter(), onEnterTransitionDidFinish(), onExit() and onExitTransitionDidStart() methods, which is very important. If you forget, you will often find that your scene behaves strangely and will not accept any touch input.

Each scene is the root node of the node hierarchy, and as such all the nodes visible on screen are children of the scene. This hierarchy is called the **scene graph**. The scene itself is an invisible node that is used as a container for all the other nodes. The following diagram shows multiple different scenes and scene graphs in a typical game:

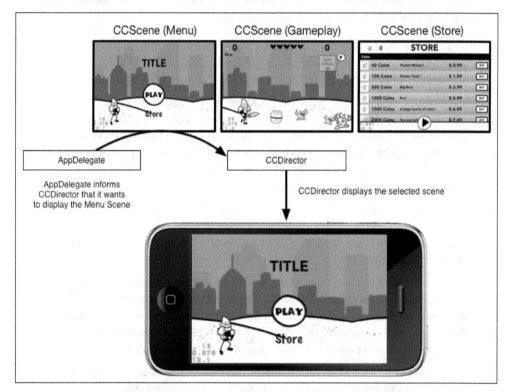

https://www.makeschool.com/docs/?source=mgwu#!/cocos2d/1.3/concepts/cocos2d-scenes-and-layers

The preceding diagram shows three separate scenes with each containing multiple nodes. It also shows how the game is created and transitioned using the AppDelegate and the CCDirector objects.

The CCDirector object is the instance that controls which scene is the current active scene and which scene is presented on screen. You can only present one scene at a time. The CCDirector is also responsible for passing on the update methods and any other scheduled methods. It also works out where to pass touch inputs when they are received.

Also seen in the diagram is the logical grouping of objects inside their scenes. It makes sense to group all the menu logic inside one scene, the game logic inside another scene, and the store inside a third scene. This keeps your game much more manageable and allows you to be flexible in the future. Let's say you decide to add an extra level to your game after the first one, you could simply insert another scene after the gameplay scene and then transition from there into the store scene.

Creating a CCScene

The CCDirector object manages the transition between scenes. To initialize your scene, you use one of two methods depending on whether your scene was created in SpriteBuilder or code.

- To initialize a scene that was created in SpriteBuilder, use the following code:

  ```
  CCScene *nextScene = [CCBReader loadAsScene:@"MyScene"];
  ```

- To initialize a scene that was created in code, use the following:

  ```
  CCScene *nextScene = * [NextScene scene];
  ```

Transitioning to another scene

To transition to another scene, you must call the CCDirector class instance. The easiest way is as follows:

```
[[CCDirector sharedDirector] replaceScene:nextScene];
```

This method will replace the current active scene with the next scene. The current active scene will then be removed from memory. Sometimes, this is not what you want. Take for example, a pause scene. You simply want this scene to appear temporarily, and then return to the gameplay scene. There are other methods provided by CCDirector to handle situations like this. The methods available are as follows:

- replaceScene: This method simply replaces the current active scene with the scene provided. The current scene is removed from memory.

- pushScene: This method pushes the next scene to the stack and makes it the current active scene. The previous scene remains in memory.

- `popScene`: This method removes the current active scene from memory and makes the previously pushed scene as the new active scene.

- `popToRootScene`: This method pops to the root node in the scene stack. It removes all other scenes from memory, and is useful to return back to a main menu button.

Care must be taken when using the `pushScene` method as it can be memory intensive. It is generally only used for temporary scenes such as pause scenes.

To animate to the next scene, all scene methods on `CCDirector` can be suffixed with the `withTransition` parameter as follows:

```
CCTransition *transition = [CCTransition transitionCrossFadeWithDurat
ion:1.0f];
[[CCDirector sharedDirector] replaceScene:nextScene
withTransition:transition];
```

There are many transitions available for use.

- `TransitionCrossFadeWithDuration`

- `TransitionFadeWithColor:duration`

- `TransitionFadeWithDuration`

- `TransitionMoveInWithDirection:duration`

- `TransitionPushWithDirection:duration`

- `TransitionRevealWithDirection:duration`

Putting it into practice

To put all your new scene knowledge into practice, you will now add a menu scene to your water bucket game. The first step is to create the class files. In Xcode, add a new class, call it `MenuScene`, and make it a subclass of `CCScene`.

The first step in creating any scene is to add the `scene` convenience method. Add the following to your class file. You might find it easier to copy, paste, and edit the equivalent method from your `IntroScene` class:

```
// -----------------------------------------------------------------
-----
#pragma mark - Create & Destroy
// -----------------------------------------------------------------
-----

+ (MenuScene *)scene
{
```

```
        return [[self alloc] init];
    }
```

This method is simply convenient as it makes creating a new scene easier.

Go to your header file and add a method stub for `scene` to make it accessible from outside this class. Your header should now look like the following:

```
#import <Foundation/Foundation.h>
#import "cocos2d.h"

@interface MenuScene : CCScene {

}
+ (MenuScene *)scene;
@end
```

Next, you need to initialize the menu scene. Add the following `init` method:

```
- (instancetype)init
{
    self = [super init];
    if (self) {
        CCPositionType positionType = CCPositionTypeMa
ke(CCPositionUnitNormalized, CCPositionUnitNormalized,
CCPositionReferenceCornerBottomLeft);
        CCButton *button = [CCButton buttonWithTitle:@"Start"];
        button.positionType = positionType;
        button.position = ccp(0.5, 0.5);
        [button setBlock:^(id sender) {
            [[CCDirector sharedDirector] pushScene:[IntroScene scene]
withTransition:[CCTransition transitionFadeWithDuration:0.33]];
        }];
        [self addChild:button];
    }
    return self;
}
```

The scene will be using a button to kick off the transition to the next scene. An Objective-C block is set to be run when the button is tapped. Inside the block, the `CCDirector` is told to push your game scene. It uses a transition to fade to the next scene with a duration of `0.33`. You could use any transition here that you want.

If you run your game now, you will see nothing has changed. First, you need to tell the director which scene to use at the apps start-up.

Open up your `AppDelegate.m` file and find the `startScene` method. Replace it with the following code:

```
-(CCScene *)startScene
{
    // This method should return the very first scene to be run when
your app starts.
    return [MenuScene scene];
}
```

Don't forget to also add an import statement for the `MenuScene` header. This method tells the director which scene is the first scene in your game.

Now, if you build and run the app, you will see a very simple menu scene. Tapping on the **Start** button loads up your game.

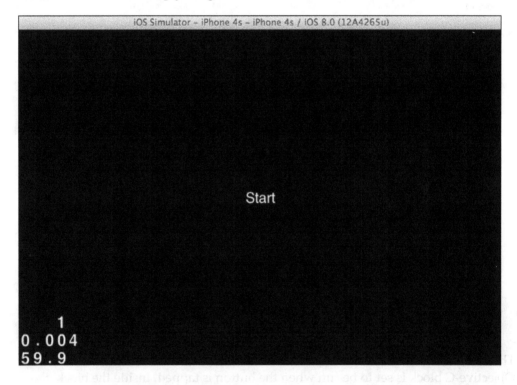

If you want, you can practice your new skills from this chapter and make this scene look a bit better. Perhaps add some sprites and change the font of the **Start** button.

Summary

You now have a basic knowledge of Cocos2d and have created your first game! You know about CCNode and the scene graph. You learned the common CCNode subclasses, including CCSprite for 2D images, CCButton for buttons, and CCLabelTTF for text. You also learned how to organize your game into different scenes using CCScene and, how to transition between these scenes using the CCDirector-shared instance. You also learned how to run code on every frame by using the update methods provided in CCNode.

In the next chapter, you will discover how you can avoid all the repetitive initialization code by using the graphical editor: SpriteBuilder.

3
SpriteBuilder

It's time to introduce you to the graphical editor that can be used with Cocos2d, **SpriteBuilder**. SpriteBuilder is a fully featured graphical development environment for Cocos2d. It is very powerful and much of your game can actually be created inside of SpriteBuilder. It is especially good at eliminating tedious and repetitive layout code because you can lay out your entire scene graphically and see the results straightaway.

In this chapter, you will learn about:

- Setting up a new project in SpriteBuilder
- The basics of SpriteBuilder
- Laying out a scene
- Animating a scene
- Transitioning between scenes

In this chapter, the basics of SpriteBuilder will be introduced as well as some simple physics. You will learn how to create a new project and set up two scenes (one for the main menu, and one for the gameplay). You will then learn how to create code connections in order to write code for your nodes that are created within SpriteBuilder. This will be accomplished by making a simple **Flappy Bird** like game entirely from CCColorNode. In order to make your Flappy Bird clone authentic, you will add some simple physics to make your character fly and detect collisions.

If you haven't already installed SpriteBuilder, you will need to install it from the Mac App Store.

Creating a new project

You will now create your first SpriteBuilder project. This will be used to make a Flappy Bird style game. SpriteBuilder is very easy to use, and a lot of people find it much easier to design their game scenes compared to writing code. The steps to create a SpriteBuilder project are as follows:

1. To start, first open SpriteBuilder. Create a new project by clicking **File | New | Project**. Call your game whatever you like, in this example `FlappySquare` was used. You should now see a screen like the following screenshot:

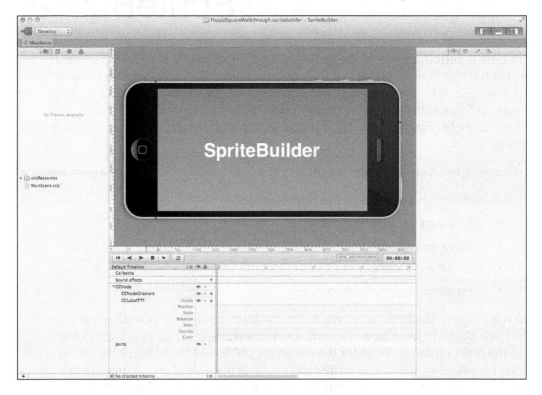

    This is the default project template for SpriteBuilder. It is a simple app that will appear on your device just as shown in the preview window in the center of the screen.

2. To build and run a SpriteBuilder app, you need to publish the project on Xcode and build and run it from there like normal. SpriteBuilder projects maintain their own internal Xcode project and to create or update it, you use the **Publish** button. The **Publish** button is located at the top-left corner next to the **Develop** drop-down menu.

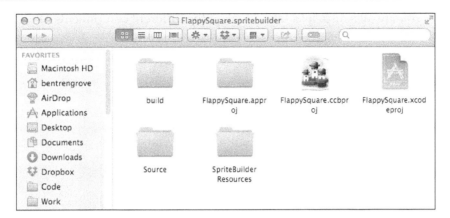

3. Press the **Publish** button. Your app will now be published on Xcode.

4. Navigate to **Finder** where you saved your SpriteBuilder project and open the folder. Inside the folder, you will see an Xcode project.

5. Open this Xcode project.

6. Build and run the project on your device. You should see an app that looks like the following screenshot:

Congratulations! You have successfully built an app from SpriteBuilder.

Now that you are all setup, let's take a look at the different components of SpriteBuilder.

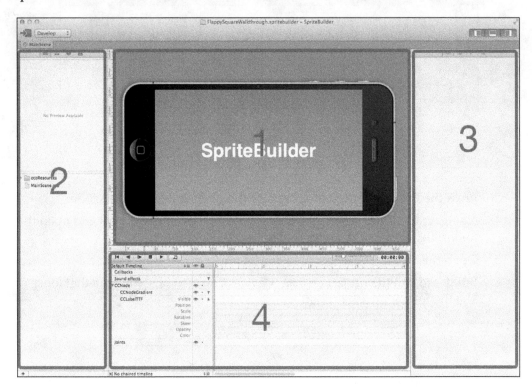

There are four major sections of SpriteBuilder:

1. The Main editor.
2. The Resource pane.
3. The Options pane.
4. The Timeline pane.

The Main editor window

The main area of SpriteBuilder is the center window. It is where all your layout happens and provides a view of what it will look like on a device. It is fully interactive; you can tap on any item you see in the device in order to select it to edit. You can also drag the items around.

Try it now; drag the SpriteBuilder label up at the top of the screen.

The Resource pane

The resource pane is where all your game objects and project resources are listed and ready to drop right into the scene. It has four sections. Tap on the third section to bring up the Object library.

The Object library is where you drag Cocos2d objects from. Everything you need to layout your scenes from simple nodes is here.

The Options pane

The options pane is where the properties of your objects can be modified. It is very similar to Interface Builder in Xcode.

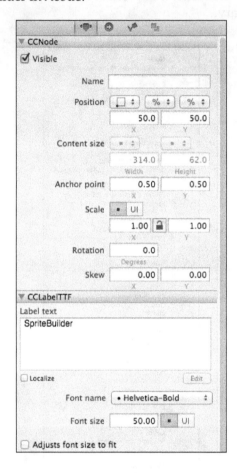

Select the SpriteBuilder logo in the main window and you will see all of its properties appear in the options pane. Here you can set the position, anchor point, scale, content size and skew all without writing any code.

You can also edit the properties of the different types of nodes. In the current case, you can set the text, font, and size of the label.

Change the label to Flappy Square.

The Timeline pane

The timeline pane is where animations are implemented. We won't be using it in this chapter and will be covering it in detail in the next chapter. For now, it can also be used as a convenient list of nodes and their hierarchy in the scene.

Creating Flappy Square

Let's start creating what is sure to be the next big hit on the App Store: Flappy Square. Flappy Square is a Flappy Bird clone that uses squares instead of fancy graphics. Don't worry! you will add some proper assets in the next chapter.

You should currently have a screen that looks like the following screenshot; if you don't move your label so it is in the same position and change its text:

1. This screen will be the menu scene of the app. Let's add a button so that players can actually start the game.

2. Drag a button from the left-hand side of SpriteBuilder onto your scene.

3. Position the button at the center of the scene and change its text to Start Game.

4. Now to add the code that will run when this button is pressed, you need to add a code connection.

5. In the options pane, open the second tab on the right-hand side of the screen. In the field marked selector, type `start`.

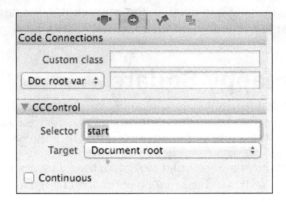

6. This is the method that Cocos2d will attempt to call when you tap on the button. Currently, this method does not exist and the game would crash. Let's add the method now.

7. Publish your SpriteBuilder project and switch to Xcode.

8. Open the `MainScene.m` file. It should just be a blank implementation.

9. Add the following method to your implementation:

```
- (void)start {
    CCLOG(@"Start tapped");
}
```

10. Build and run your game.

11. You should see your button on screen. Tapping on this button produces a console message.

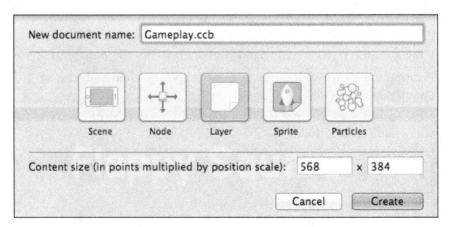

Creating a new scene/layer

You now need to link a scene to the app when the user taps on start. This new scene will be the gameplay scene of your app. Following are the steps:

1. To create a new scene in SpriteBuilder, click on **File** | **New** | **File**. This will open up the **New File** dialog box.

2. Name your new document `Gameplay.ccb` and select **Layer**. The reason you will select layer rather than scene is because you will need to be able to position objects outside the screen. Scenes present in the iPhone border around the main window. Layers allow you to add objects to any position regardless of its layer content size.

3. You will now see an empty black layer. Let's make it look a bit nicer.

4. Open the Object library (third tab on the left-hand side of the screen). Using `CCColorNodes` from the library, decorate your layer to look like sky and ground. You can also use `CCGradientNodes` to fill a square with a gradient.

5. You can use the options pane on the right-hand side of the screen to configure your nodes, or you can use the click-and-drag modifiers in the main window.

6. Once you have created a ground and sky for your layer, add another **CCNodeColor** of size (30, 30). Set the new nodes color to one that will stand out. After you have finished creating your layer, it should look something like the following image. Don't worry if it's a little different, these nodes are just for looks.

Linking to a SpriteBuilder scene in code

Now that you have created your layer, you need to link it in code. This will allow you to transition to the new scene when the user presses the start button. In order to do this, you need to let Cocos2d know which class in code to associate the scene with.

1. In the timeline view, select the topmost option: **CCNode**.

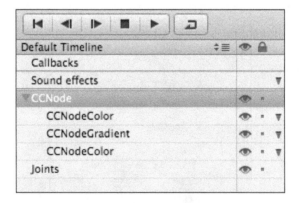

2. Now, select the **Code Connection** pane on the right-hand side of the screen. It is the second tab. Create a **Custom class** named `Gameplay` in `CCNode`.

3. Now, open Xcode again and create a new `CCNode` subclass named `Gameplay`. Make sure to save it in the source folder to keep your project structure consistent.

4. The new class you just represented is the class file for your layer in SpriteBuilder. They are linked with the name you typed in the **Custom class** field.

5. Switch back to `MainScene.m` and replace the start method with the following code:

```
- (void)start {
    CCScene *gameplay = [CCBReader loadAsScene:@"Gameplay"];
    [[CCDirector sharedDirector] pushScene:gameplay
withTransition:[CCTransition transitionFadeWithDuration:0.33]];
}
```

6. Build and run your game. You should see a nicely rendered version of the layer you designed in SpriteBuilder.

Enabling physics in SpriteBuilder

In the current game, you want your character, the small square, to fall to the ground and stop. Later on, you will introduce the flapping mechanic, but for now, let's keep it simple.

Everything that is to have physics applied to it in Cocos2d must be a child of CCPhysicsNode. Luckily, SpriteBuilder makes this very simple by including physics nodes in the Object library. Following are the steps:

1. Open the Object library again and drag out a physics node. Position it at (0, 0). Also, increase the gravity property to (0, -700).

2. You now need to make any object that is included in the physics simulation a child of this physics node. In your current app, this is the character square and the ground.

3. In SpriteBuilder, you can reorganize the node hierarchy by simply dragging the nodes in the timeline editor. Drag your character node and ground node from the top of the physics node into the timeline editor. They will then become children of the physics node.

4. There is no need to worry about the sky node as it is not part of the simulation.

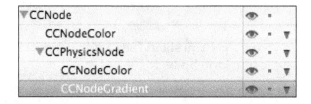

5. Now you need to set up the physics engine. The desired behavior is that the ground never moves, and the character falls down and lands on the ground.

6. First, you need to enable physics for both objects. The physics options are configured in the third tab in the options pane.

7. Click on each object one at a time **Enable physics** in the physics options pane.

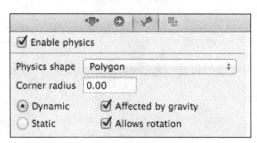

8. Now, in order to make the ground never move, it needs to become static. Edit the physics options for the ground and select **Static**. It ensures that the object never moves; it simply can be interacted with by other objects.

9. Publish your game to Xcode. Build and run the game and see what happens.

You should see your character square fall down and stop on the ground. You now see the power of SpriteBuilder. Without any code in your gameplay scene, you have enabled physics and set up a physics simulation.

Connecting SpriteBuilder objects to Xcode properties

It's now time to make your character fly. When the user taps on the screen, the character will jump up again. In order to do this, you will have to write some code. In order to write code, you are going to need a reference to the character square. To do this, you create a new code connection. Instead of setting up a custom class, this time you are going to link a node to a property of the Gameplay.m class. Following are the steps:

1. Select your character square in SpriteBuilder and open the **Code Connection** options. In the field named **Doc root var**, type _character.

2. Publish it on Xcode and open your Xcode project.

3. Add a private interface at the top of your Gameplay.m file. Inside this file, create a CCNode property named character:

   ```
   @interface Gameplay()

   @property (nonatomic) CCNode *character;

   @end
   ```

4. Add a new method flap and type in the following code.

   ```
   - (void)flap {
       CGPoint forceDirection = ccp(0.0, 1.0);
       CGPoint impulse = ccpMult(forceDirection, 800);
       [self.character.physicsBody applyImpulse:impulse];
   }
   ```

5. To make your character flap, an impulse will be applied. The direction is upwards and this is multiplied with the magnitude.

6. This impulse is applied to the physics body of your character. More information about this will be covered in *Chapter 6, Physics Engines*.

7. Now, you need to call this method on touch. Add the following code:

```
- (void)didLoadFromCCB
{
    self.userInteractionEnabled = YES;
}
- (void)touchBegan:(UITouch *)touch withEvent:(UIEvent *)event {
    [self flap];
}
```

Instead of the `init` method, the `didLoadFromCCB` method is used. This method is called when the scene has been successfully unpacked from the SpriteBuilder file, and all the code connections are now available for use.

8. Build and run the game now. You should be able to tap on the screen and make your character jump upwards.

9. You might notice that there is a problem; if you tap too often, the character shoots out quickly from the top of the screen. In order to counter this, you will need to limit the velocity of the node.

10. This will be achieved with the `update` method. Add the following method:

```
- (void)update:(CCTime)delta {
    // clamp velocity
    CGFloat yVelocity = clampf(self.character.physicsBody.
velocity.y, -1 * MAXFLOAT, 200.f);
    self.character.physicsBody.velocity = ccp(0, yVelocity);
}
```

 Recall from *Chapter 2, Nodes, Sprites, and Scenes* that the `update` method is called on every frame.

11. Build and run the game now. You should have a smoothly flying square.

Creating reusable components

Now that your game has a flapping square, it would be nice to have some obstacles. As you want more than one obstacle, it would be nice to create a component that could be reused multiple times. SpriteBuilder makes this process simple. Following are the steps:

1. Reopen your SpriteBuilder project and create a new file. This time, instead of a layer, create node. Name the node `Obstacle`.

2. Drag two `CCNodeColor` objects onto the main window. Set both their sizes to (40, 300). Set their colors to whatever you like. Position one node at (0, 0), and the other node at (0, 425). Enable physics on both nodes and set their physics type to **Static**.

3. Select the parent `CCNode` from the timeline editor. Set its content size to (40, 725). Set a Custom class for the node to `Obstacle`.

4. Your SpriteBuilder should now look like the following screenshot:

5. This new object will be your obstacle in your game.

6. Reopen the **Gameplay** file.

7. Open the Object library. Drag a **Sub File** on top of the physics node. In the options pane, select the `CCB` file as `Obstacle.ccb`. Position your obstacle at a good starting point.

8. Your scene should now look like the following screenshot:

The **Sub File** component of SpriteBuilder is one of the most powerful features. It allows you to create reusable components in your games.

9. Create two more obstacle subfiles and evenly space them at the right-hand side of the first obstacle.

10. Create a Doc root var code connection for each obstacle. Name them _obstacle1, _obstacle2, and _obstacle3, respectively.

Moving obstacles across the screen

Now, you need to move the obstacles across the screen. To do this, you will need to reference them in code:

1. Publish and switch over to Xcode. Add the following properties to your private interface:

   ```
   @property (nonatomic) NSMutableArray *obstacles;
   @property (nonatomic) CCNode *obstacle1;
   @property (nonatomic) CCNode *obstacle2;
   @property (nonatomic) CCNode *obstacle3;
   ```

2. Also, add the following line to your didLoadFromCCB method:

   ```
   self.obstacles = [NSMutableArray arrayWithObjects:self.obstacle1,
   self.obstacle2, self.obstacle3, nil];
   ```

3. Now, to actually move these across screen, add the following code underneath the velocity clamp in the `update` method:

```
//Move the obstacles across the screen
for (CCNode *obstacle in self.obstacles) {
    obstacle.position = ccpSub(obstacle.position, ccp(3.0,
0));

    //Check if they have gone off screen, if they have
reposition them
    if (obstacle.position.x < -obstacle.contentSize.width) {
        int y = -(arc4random_uniform(180)+70);
        obstacle.position = ccp(self.boundingBox.size.width *
2, y);
    }
}
```

4. Also, as you added a custom class to your `Obstacle` subfile, you will need to create the corresponding code file or else the game will crash.

5. Create a new `CCNode` subclass called `Obstacle`.

6. Build and run your game.

You should now have an endless supply of obstacles to try and dodge. The only problem is that nothing happens when you actually hit one.

Detecting collisions

The last thing missing from Flappy Square is the end condition. When your character squares hit an obstacle, the game should end. This will be achieved by detecting a collision between each of the obstacle squares and the character square. Following are the steps:

1. First, you need to add code connections to the obstacle squares so that code can be written for them.

2. Open SpriteBuilder, and then open the `Obstacle.ccb` file.

3. Add a code connection to each block named `_bottomBlock` and `_topBlock`, respectively.

4. Publish and switch back to Xcode. Open the `Obstacle.m` file and add the properties for the blocks:

```
@interface Obstacle()
@property (nonatomic) CCNode *topBlock;
@property (nonatomic) CCNode *bottomBlock;
```

```
@end
```
Also add the following method:
```
- (void)didLoadFromCCB {
    self.topBlock.physicsBody.collisionType = @"obstacle";
    self.topBlock.physicsBody.sensor = YES;
    self.bottomBlock.physicsBody.collisionType = @"obstacle";
    self.bottomBlock.physicsBody.sensor = YES;
}
```

Setting the physics body sensor property to `true` makes objects that collide with that physics body unaffected. It simply gives you a chance at a callback to let you know that the collision has happened. It is very good for invisible objects, for example, to check whether you wanted to detect when an object entered a region.

1. Open your `Gameplay.m` file again.

2. Change your interface to adopt the `Collision` delegate:
```
@interface Gameplay() <CCPhysicsCollisionDelegate>
```
   This protocol defines the methods for use when detecting collisions. The delegate is set on the physics node, so you will need to add a code connection for it.

3. Open your SpriteBuilder project and add a code connection to the physics node. Name it _physicsRootNode.

4. Add the corresponding property to your `Gameplay.m` file:
```
@property (nonatomic) CCPhysicsNode *physicsRootNode;
```

5. Add the following lines to your `didLoadFromCCB` method:
```
self.physicsRootNode.collisionDelegate = self;
self.character.physicsBody.collisionType = @"character";
```

6. Now, in order to detect the collision between an obstacle and a character, you need to implement the correct method. Add the following code at the bottom of your `Gameplay.m` file:
```
- (BOOL)ccPhysicsCollisionBegin:(CCPhysicsCollisionPair *)pair
character:(CCNode *)nodeA obstacle:(CCNode *)nodeB {
    CCLOG(@"Game over");
    [[CCDirector sharedDirector] popScene];
    return YES;
}
```
   Notice that the parameter name for nodeA and nodeB is character and obstacle, respectively. The Cocos2d physics engine looks to see whether the delegate implements a method with the names of the `collisionTypes` property. If it does, it will call this method.

7. Build and run your game now. You should see a complete, but very basic Flappy Square game.

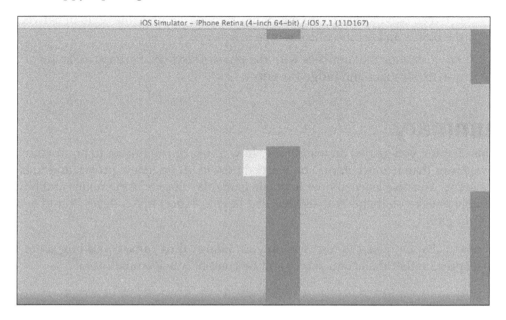

When your character collides with an obstacle, the game drops back to the main menu.

The next step

Now, you have seen the power of SpriteBuilder. With a relatively small amount of code, you have created a game that has complex physics mechanics. There was no layout code to write at all which keeps the code very readable.

You learned a lot in this chapter. SpriteBuilder is a large piece of software and you require a lot of practice to learn it properly. You should now have a basic understanding about how to layout a scene, and how to create resuseable components to speed up developer. Reuseable components also cut down on code repetition.

Of course! The game is very simple and lacks polish. In the next chapter, you will add some proper assets and design simple animations to go with them. You will also learn about **particle systems**. This will take the game to a whole new level.

In the meantime, however you could think about adding the following features:

1. Add a score system. You will need to detect when the character passes between two blocks. To do this, you could use an invisible node in between the blocks and set its collision type to sensor.

2. Try to change the numbers with the physics settings. Perhaps make the gravity stronger and judge the effect.

Summary

In this chapter, you gained an insight into how to use SpriteBuilder to build your games faster than it was before. You learned how to set up a new project and to lay out a scene. You also learned how to create gameplay objects using nodes and how to enable physics on them. You also learned how to export to Xcode and build and run your game.

In the next chapter, you will improve on your Flappy Bird game by adding some actual sprites rather than color nodes and by creating some animations.

4
Animation with SpriteBuilder

In the previous chapter, you were introduced to SpriteBuilder. In order to keep it simple, the tutorial did not use any graphical assets. In this chapter, you will learn how to add assets to SpriteBuilder and create animations for them. It will really take your Flappy Bird game to the next level. You will also be introduced to particles to add a nice little effect to the bird when the user taps the screen.

The following points will be covered in this chapter:

- Adding sprite assets to SpriteBuilder
- Animating in SpriteBuilder using sprite frames
- Animating nodes in SpriteBuilder using keyframes
- Animating in code using actions
    - Moving, scaling, and rotating
    - Sequencing actions
    - Delaying actions
    - Running actions at the same time
    - Repeating actions
    - Running code with actions to get a callback

Adding sprites to SpriteBuilder

Just using basic shapes does not create the best looking game. In order to make your game better, you will now learn how to add real assets to your game.

First, you will need to acquire some assets. You can create your own if you like or download some premade assets from `https://s3.amazonaws.com/mgwu-misc/ Spritebuilder+Tutorial/PeevedPenguinsAssets.zip`.

If you are looking for more game art, you can check out
OpenGameArt.org for some great assets.

Open up your project from the last chapter in SpriteBuilder. To import assets into
SpriteBuilder, you need to drag them into the resources pane on the left. Drag in the
asset files now. You should now see them listed in the resources pane.

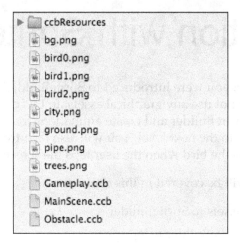

You may notice that you do not have different assets for retina and non-retina. This
is because SpriteBuilder automatically converts them for you. You just have to let
it know what it is starting with. The default starting scale is 4x, but the images you
have imported are at the 2x size. To change this setting, perform the following:

1. Open up **Project Settings** by clicking **File | Project Settings**.

2. Change the **Default scaling from** setting to **2x (phonehd)**.

When publishing, SpriteBuilder will automatically resize these images for you. Having lots of separate images however is bad for performance as it greatly increases the overhead. Loading files from the disk takes time, and for each file, there is an overhead. To overcome this problem, many graphics engines, including Cocos2d, have support for **sprite sheets**. Sprite sheets pack all your small graphic assets into one large file. The implementation is completely hidden from the programmer. You still use the assets as if they were single files but you get the extra performance benefits.

In order to enable this feature, you need to separate your assets into folders. In large games, you can make folders for each part of your game. Perhaps, you can make one per screen or level and one for common assets across all screens. In your game, there aren't too many assets, so one folder will be fine. Following are the steps:

1. To create the folder, right-click on the resources area and create a new folder. Call it whatever you choose. Then, drag all the game assets into this folder.

2. Next, right-click on the folder and select **Make Smart Sprite Sheet**.

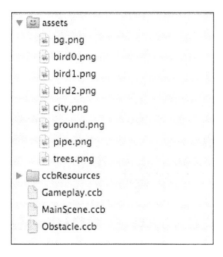

Let's see the results of this:

3. Click **Publish**.

4. Navigate to your SpriteBuilder project resources in **Finder**.

There will be a new file that is an image of all your assets combined.

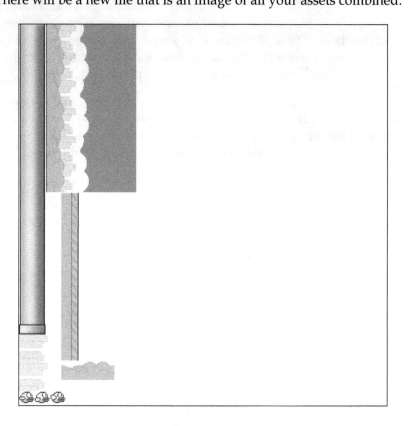

Creating sprite frame animations

You may have noticed that there are three assets for the bird. These will be used to create a keyframe animation that will run in a loop. SpriteBuilder makes this process very simple:

1. Create a new file that uses a sprite as its root object. Call it `Bird`.

2. Select **CSprite** in the editor.

3. In the options pane on the right-hand side of the screen, there is an option for **Sprite frame**. Set it to `bird0.png`.

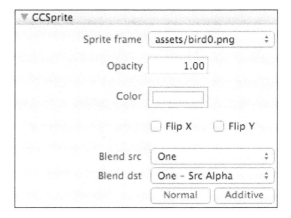

4. Now, in order to create the animation, select all the bird images in the resources pane on the left of the screen. Right-click on them and select **Create keyframes from Selection**.

5. Notice that there has been three keyframes created in the timeline editor. If you click play, you will notice that the bird quickly flaps and then gets stuck on the last frame while the rest of the timeline plays out.

6. In order to fix this, you need to set the timeline duration. Open the options for the default timeline and select **Set timeline duration**. Enter 0 seconds and 3 frames.

7. You also have to set up the animation to loop. This is accomplished with the chaining of timelines. In order to create a loop, you simply chain the timeline to itself.

8. At the bottom of the timeline, there is an option currently set to **No chained timeline**. Click on this and select **Default Timeline**.

9. Your bird sprite animation is now complete. Let's drop it in the main menu in order to see it in action.

10. Open your `MainScene.ccb` file and drop in a subfile node. Select your `Bird.ccb file` as the **CCB File**.

 If nothing appears after selecting `Bird.ccb`, make sure you have saved your bird file.

We can now also switch out the square in the game play scene with your new bird subfile.

11. Open your `Gameplay` layer.

12. Delete the square and drag out a new subfile onto the physics node in the timeline.

 Remember to re-add the code connection a `doc root` var named `_character` and enable physics.

13. Change the physics shape to **circle** as it better fits the image of our bird.

14. Publish your game and run it from Xcode.

You now have a real flapping bird!

Switching out the obstacle image

Knowing that you cleverly made your obstacle a separate subfile, it is very easy to switch in the image of the pipe. Let's do this now:

1. Open up the `Obstacle` file and delete the two red squares.

2. Drag out two images of the pipe from the resources tab.

3. You will have to rotate one of them to 180 degrees so that it is facing the correct direction. Line them up where the red blocks were.

4. You will also have to re-add your code connections and physics so the collisions work.

5. Enable physics on both and set the physics type to be **Polygon** and **Static**. Also, add the `doc root var` code connections `_topBlock` and `_bottomBlock`, respectively.

6. Open the `Gameplay` scene and drag out some ground sprites to replace your gradient node ground. You will probably have to overlap two of them. Ensure that your new ground nodes have physics enabled and are children of the physics node in the scene.

7. Also drag out some background images to make your scene look good.

8. Publish and run the game and have a look!

The game is starting to look really good now.

Particle systems

A great item of polish that could be added to your game is a particle system. Particle systems can be designed right in SpriteBuilder with the fully featured particle system editor. If you are unsure of what a particle system is, then the best way to learn is by having a look.

In your Flappy Bird project, create a new file. Select **Particles** and name it `FlapParticles`.

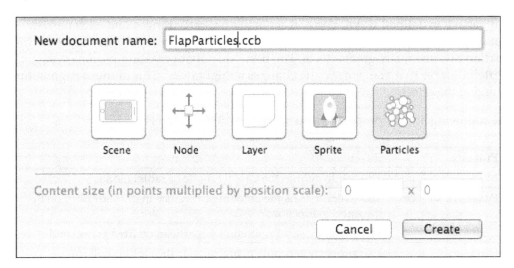

You should see a new file open up with what looks like a flame in the center of the screen:

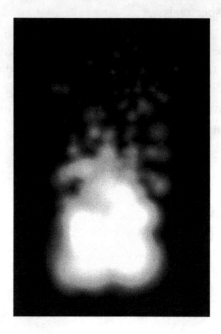

This is a particle system. Particle systems allow the spawning of many small sprites that behave in defined ways. You can set many property ranges and each particle that is spawned will be randomly assigned a value in that range. This allows for the creation of some really great effects. The best thing about creating particle systems in SpriteBuilder is that you can see the changes straightaway. This allows for great fine tuning of the effect.

The following are the properties you can edit and their effects:

Property	Effect
Mode	This mode defines the Gravity mode or radial mode.
Position Variance	This property sets the amount of variance in the start position in the x and y direction.
Emit Rate	This property sets the amount of particles emitted per second
Duration	This property sets how many seconds the emitter will run. -1 means forever.
Total Particles	This property sets a maximum number of particles to exist at a time.
Life	This property sets the amount of seconds each particle lives. You can also set a variance for this property.

Start Size	This property sets how big the particles start their life. You can also set a variance for this property.
End Size	This property sets how big the particles are at the end of their life. You can also set a variance for this property.
Start Spin	This property defines how much rotation/ spin a particle has at the start of its life. You can also set a variance for this property.
End Spin	This property defines how much rotation / spin a particle has at the end of its life. You can also set a variance for this property.
Angle	This property sets the angle of the entire particle system. This is used to control the direction of the particles emitted. You can also set a variance for this property.
Start Color	This property sets the starting color of the particle.
End Color	This property sets the end color of the particle.

The particle system can be set into one of two modes, Gravity or Radial.

The Gravity mode is the default mode that produces particle systems like the one SpriteBuilder defaults to. An example of particles in the gravity mode is shown as follows:

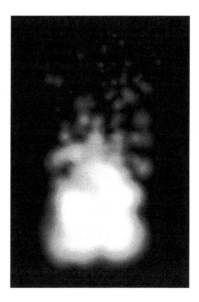

Gravity mode has a few unique settings:

Property	Effect
Gravity	This property defines the direction of gravity.
Speed	This property defines the strength of the gravity.
Tangential Acceleration	This property defines the acceleration tangential to the direction of the particle.
Radial Acceleration	This property defines the acceleration in the radial direction. The radial direction is perpendicular to the tangential acceleration.

The Radial mode produces what could be described as a black hole sort of effect, as seen in the following screenshot:

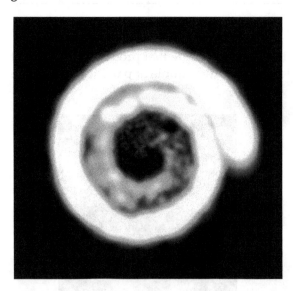

Property	Effect
Start Radius	This property sets how wide the radius of rotation is at the start. You can also set a variance for this property.
End Radius	This property sets how wide the radius is at the end. You can also set a variance for this property.
Rotate	This property sets the angle of rotation per second.

Designing a particle system for our character

Using the tools in SpriteBuilder, you will now create a simple particle effect for when the bird character flaps their wings.

Have a go at designing one yourself. For reference, here is what is used in the example code:

Property	Effect
Mode	Gravity
Position Variance	0,0
Emit rate	25
Duration	0.25
Total Particles	6
Life	0.25 +/- 0.15
Start size	5 +/- 1
End Size	5 +/- 1
Start Spin	0
End Spin	0
Angle	180 +/- 90
Start Color	Brown
End Color	Brown

For gravity, the following settings were used:

Property	Effect
Gravity	(-100, 0)
Speed	10 +/- 20
Tangential Acceleration	0
Radial Acceleration	100 +/- 50

Adding a SpriteBuilder particle system in code

Now that you have designed your particle system, you need to add it into your code. It shall be fired when the bird flaps.

1. Publish your SpriteBuilder project and open up your Xcode project and navigate to the Gameplay.m file. Modify the file to look as follows:

```
CCParticleSystem *explosion = (CCParticleSystem *)[CCBReader
load:@"FlapParticles"];
// make the particle effect clean itself up, once it is
completed
explosion.autoRemoveOnFinish = TRUE;
// place the particle effect on the characters
explosion.position = self.character.position;
// add the particle effect to the same parent as the character
[self.character.parent addChild:explosion];
```

2. Build and run your game. You should now see a small particle effect when the bird flaps.

Final polish to Flappy Bird

As one final touch of polish to your game, you need to make the bird rotate towards the ground as it flies. This gives a great more natural flying effect.

To do this, you will need to keep track of how long it has been since the last touch and rotate the bird accordingly:

1. Add a new property to your gameplay.m file:

```
@property (assign) CGFloat timeSinceLastTouch;
```

2. In your touchBegan method, set it to zero:

```
- (void)touchBegan:(UITouch *)touch withEvent:(UIEvent *)event {
    [self flap];

    self.timeSinceLastTouch = 0.0f;
}
```

3. Now, navigate to your `update` method. Add the following code:

```
//Keep track of the time since the last touch
self.timeSinceLastTouch += delta;
//Set the new rotation of our character to be in a range
    self.character.rotation = clampf(self.character.rotation,
-30.f, 90.f);
    if (self.character.physicsBody.allowsRotation) {
//Apply a rotation force to generate a smooth rotation
        float angularVelocity = clampf(self.character.physicsBody.
angularVelocity, -2.f, 1.f);
        self.character.physicsBody.angularVelocity =
angularVelocity;
    }
    if ((self.timeSinceLastTouch > 0.5f)) {
        [self.character.physicsBody applyAngularImpulse:-
40000.f*delta];
    }
```

4. Also navigate to your `flap` method and add this line underneath where you apply the impulse:

```
[self.character.physicsBody applyAngularImpulse:10000.f];
```

5. Build and run your game. You should now have a nicely rotating bird.

Keyframe animation in SpriteBuilder

Animations can also be created in SpriteBuilder with keyframes. In the SpriteBuilder timeline, there is a full keyframe animation editor. Each node can have multiple properties animated.

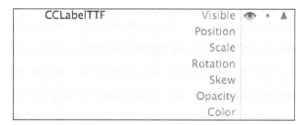

Keyframe animation works by setting a keyframe on the starting value and then later in the timeline, a keyframe is set for the ending value. The animation then automatically advances between these values.

It is easier to understand in practice:

1. Open your main menu scene in SpriteBuilder. Drag out a `Bird.ccb` subfile. You will create an animation to move the bird from offscreen to the center of the screen.

2. Drag the bird out of the scene to where it will start its animation.

3. Now, you need to set a key frame for the starting position. Ensure your timeline is set to zero by dragging the blue bar in the timeline back to the start.

4. With your bird node selected, open the menu and select **Animation | Insert Keyframe | Position**:

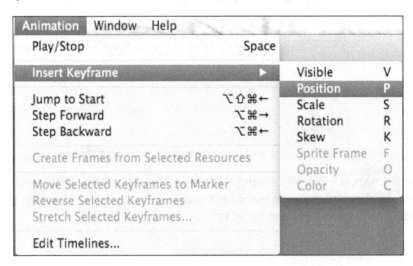

This will add a keyframe to the timeline for position.

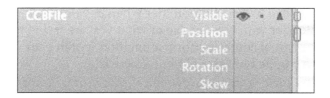

5. Now, drag your timeline bar and set it to three seconds. Move your bird node to the center of the screen. This is where your animation will finish. You will notice that SpriteBuilder has automatically inserted a new keyframe for you where you set your timeline.

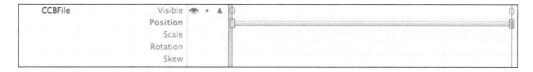

If you play the animation now, you can see the bird move onto the screen.

In order to make animations look better in almost all cases, you will want to apply some easing to the tween. We will look at all the different types of easing shortly, but in order to ease your animation in SpriteBuilder, you need to right-click on the purple bar and select an ease type.

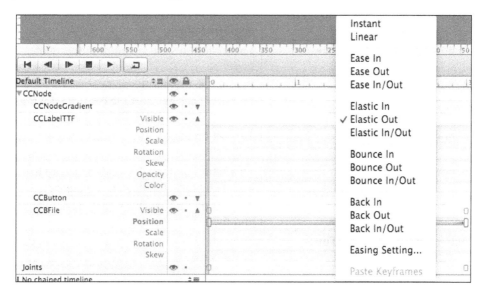

Have an experiment with the different types of easing offered by SpriteBuilder.

Animation in code

Of course, you don't have to use SpriteBuilder when developing for Cocos2d. Sometimes, SpriteBuilder won't be capable of what you are trying to achieve. For these situations, you can of course perform animation within your code. There is a powerful animation engine built straight into Cocos2d.

Moving, scaling, and rotating

In the last section, you saw how you can keep track of time since an event starter and use that knowledge in the update method to change an attribute of a node. You can write all your animation like this, but there is a much simpler way to accomplish simple animations. This method uses CCAction. By using CCAction, you can accomplish many animations, such as move, rotate, and scale.

Here is a list of CCActions available to you in code:

Action	Effect
CCActionMoveTo, CCActionMoveBy	This action moves a node to a position or by a certain amount.
CCActionJumpTo, CCActionJumpBy	This action jumps a node in a parabolic arc to a position or by a certain amount.
CCActionScaleTo, CCActionScaleBy	This action scales a node to or by a certain value.
CCActionRotateTo, CCActionRotateBy	This action rotates a node to or by a certain angle in degrees.
CCActionShow, CCActionHide	This action sets the visibility property of a node.
CCActionBlink	This action toggles the node's visibility property back and forth to cause a blinking effect.
CCActionToggleVisibility	This action toggles the node's visibility property.
CCActionFadeIn	This action first sets the node's opacity to 0 and then fades in the node to an opacity of 1.
CCActionFadeOut	This action first sets the node's opacity to 1 and then fades it out to 0.
CCActionTintBy, CCActionTintTo	This action changes the tint color of a node by or to a value.

To use an action, you simply create the action and then run it on the node as follows:

```
CCActionMoveTo *move = [CCActionMoveTo actionWithDuration:1.0
position:ccp(10, 10)];
    [self.character runAction:move];
```

By default, all actions occur over a linear time scale. Generally, this does not look good and you probably want to ease all your animations.

Imagine moving a node from the left side of the screen to the right. With a linear time scale, it will move a set amount of pixels per second, no matter where it is up to in the animation. This almost never happens in real life, normally objects accelerate and decelerate. It is for this reason, that it is generally desirable to ease your animations. Cocos2d makes this very easy to accomplish and provides a number of prebuilt easing functions for your use.

Ease actions come in three types:

- ease in
- ease out
- ease InOut

These names describe where the change of the acceleration curve happens.

The most common easing patterns are listed as follows:

- **Linear**: This is the effect of having no easing.

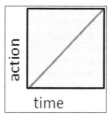

- **EaseIn**: EaseIn slows the speed at the start and then speeds up.

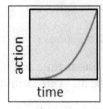

- **EaseOut**: EaseOut is the opposite of ease in. The animation will slow at the end.

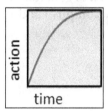

- **EaseInOut**: EaseInOut slows the animation at the start and end. It is the most commonly used `easing` function. Animations in iOS use an ease similar to this one.

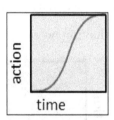

There are many easing types you can choose from. For a full list and handy demonstration of the different ease types, check out `http://kirillmuzykov.com/cocos2d-iphone-easing-examples/`.

To apply an ease function to an action, you just have to create the ease action with the original action and then run it on the node.

```
CCActionMoveTo *move = [CCActionMoveTo actionWithDuration:1.0
position:ccp(10, 10)];
CCActionEaseInOut *easedAction = [CCActionEaseInOut
actionWithAction:move];
[self.character runAction:easedAction];
```

Chaining actions together

It is very common to want to run an action at the completion of another action. For example, you may want to move a node to a position, and once it arrives, scale it up. To accomplish this, you use another type of action, the CCSequence action.

A CCActionSequence takes an array of actions and runs them one after another, in sequence. To achieve what is described above, you would use the following code:

```
    CCActionMoveTo *move = [CCActionMoveTo actionWithDuration:1.0
position:ccp(10, 10)];
    CCActionEaseInOut *easedMove = [CCActionEaseInOut
actionWithAction:move];
    CCActionScaleBy *scale = [CCActionScaleBy actionWithDuration:1.0
scale:2.0];
    CCActionEaseInOut *easedScale = [CCActionEaseInOut
actionWithAction:scale];

    CCActionSequence *sequence = [CCActionSequence actions:easedMove,
easedScale, nil];
    [self.character runAction:sequence];
```

What if you want the scale to happen after a delay? There is another action for this, CCActionDelay. To use it, you have to create the object with a duration and then simply place it in the sequence where you want it to occur:

```
    CCActionDelay *delay = [CCActionDelay actionWithDuration:1.0];
    CCActionSequence *sequence = [CCActionSequence actions:easedMove,
delay, easedScale, nil];
```

Running actions simultaneously

It is also very common to want to run actions simultaneously. This is very simple to do, just run the action one after another in code. In the following code, you shall move and scale your character node at the same time:

```
CCActionMoveTo *move = [CCActionMoveTo actionWithDuration:1.0
position:ccp(10, 10)];
    CCActionEaseInOut *easedMove = [CCActionEaseInOut
actionWithAction:move];
    CCActionScaleBy *scale = [CCActionScaleBy actionWithDuration:1.0
scale:2.0];
    CCActionEaseInOut *easedScale = [CCActionEaseInOut
actionWithAction:scale];
  [self.character runAction:easedMove];
[self.character runAction:easedScale];
```

However, there is one slight catch to this method. What if you want to use it in a sequence? For this situation, there is another type of action, CCActionSpawn. A CCActionSpawn action is like a CCActionSequence, except it runs its actions at the same time. It is created in the same manner as CCActionSequence.

```
CCActionSpawn *spawn = [CCActionSpawn actions:easedMove, easedScale,
nil];
    [self.character runAction:spawn];
```

You can also use the spawn you create inside a sequence or use a sequence inside of a spawn.

Repeating actions

Another type of action can be used to create repeating actions or actions' sequences. For instance, you may want a pulsating scale effect where a node scales up and down repeatedly. This can be accomplished with CCActionRepeat as follows:

```
    CCActionScaleTo *scaleUp = [CCActionScaleTo actionWithDuration:1.0
scale:2.0];
    CCActionScaleTo *scaleDown = [CCActionScaleTo
actionWithDuration:1.0 scale:2.0];
    CCActionSequence *scaleSeq = [CCActionSequence actions:scaleUp,
scaleDown, nil];
    CCActionRepeat *repeat = [CCActionRepeat actionWithAction:scaleSeq
times:5];
    [self.character runAction:repeat];
```

This will scale up and down your node five times.

If you want to repeat forever, there is another action for that, CCActionRepeatForever.

```
    CCActionRepeatForever *repeat = [CCActionRepeatForever
actionWithAction:scaleSeq];
```

Running code on completion of an animation

A very common requirement is to run some code on the completion of an animation. You would want to move a node off screen and then once set off screen, remove it from your scene for instance. This can be easily accomplished with another set of actions, CCActionCallBlock and CCActionCallFunc.

The most convenient to use is the block based action as it allows you to access the node that is having the action run on it:

```
    CCActionCallBlock *blockAction = [CCActionCallBlock
actionWithBlock:^{
        [self.character removeFromParent];
    }];
    CCActionSequence *blockSequence = [CCActionSequence
actions:easedMove, blockAction, nil];
    [self.character runAction:blockSequence];
```

> For Cocos2d users who used a previous version, the `CallFuncN` and `CallFuncO` actions have been removed from Cocos2d v3.0. In order to recreate their functionality, you need to use the block-based actions and access the node through local scope.

Summary

There was a lot covered in this chapter on animation. Animation is probably the most important part of game development, as without it nothing on the screen will move or change. You learned how to add assets into the SpriteBuilder so that your games will look much more polished. You then learned how to animate these assets. Of course, sometimes, SpriteBuilder can't meet all your needs; so, you also learnt how to perform animations in code.

In the next chapter, you will learn how to put together user interfaces. You will also learn about the different ways of accepting user input through touch and the accelerometer.

5
User Interaction and Interface

What good is a game when the user can't actually interact with it! User interaction is a key feature of a game and is often overlooked. In this chapter, you will learn how to take input from a wide variety of methods.

In this chapter, you will learn how to:

- Detect and respond to the user touching the screen
- Add buttons to your scene in code
- Take input from the user with form elements such as `CCTextField` and `CCSlider`
- Create a scrollable table view using `CCTableView`

Detecting touches

In Cocos2D, every `CCNode` class and subclass can receive and handle touches. You just have to enable one property. This property is the `userInteractionEnabled` property and is written as follows:

```
- (id)init
{
    if (self = [super init])
    {
        // activate touches on this scene
        self.userInteractionEnabled = YES;
    }
    return self;
}
```

Enabling this property registers your node with the touch dispatcher. There are four types of touch events. These occur:

- When touches begin
- When touches end
- When touches move
- When touches are cancelled

Using these events allows you to track any touch as it moves around the screen. These events are passed to your node by implementing the `touch` delegate methods:

```
(void)touchBegan:(UITouch *)touch withEvent:(UIEvent *)event
(void)touchMoved:(UITouch *)touch withEvent:(UIEvent *)event
(void)touchEnded:(UITouch *)touch withEvent:(UIEvent *)event
(void)touchCancelled:(UITouch *)touch withEvent:(UIEvent *)event
```

Multitouch can be enabled by setting the following property:

```
self.multipleTouchEnabled = YES;
```

If this is set, each touch will call the corresponding event method individually. If you have four fingers touching the screen, you will get four `touchBegan` calls. It is up to you to keep track of all the touches manually, this can be done by storing a strong reference to each `UITouch` object and checking which touch has moved.

Getting the touch location

Knowing that a user touched the screen is of some use, but it is very limited. What you really want to do is know where the user touched the screen.

Start a new Xcode project using the Cocos2d template. Open up `HelloWorldScene.m`. You will see that there is already a `touchBegan` method implemented:

```
-(void) touchBegan:(UITouch *)touch withEvent:(UIEvent *)event {
    CGPoint touchLoc = [touch locationInNode:self];

    // Log touch location
    CCLOG(@"Move sprite to @ %@",NSStringFromCGPoint(touchLoc));

    // Move our sprite to touch location
    CCActionMoveTo *actionMove = [CCActionMoveTo
actionWithDuration:1.0f position:touchLoc];
    [_sprite runAction:actionMove];
}
```

You will notice the first line calculates the touch location relative to the scene. Remember that if you are in a CCNode child class, the calculated touch location will be relative to that node, not the screen. You can always pass a different node into the locationInNode method to get it relative to another node.

Dragging a node

You will now learn how to drag a node using the touch information.

If you are moving along from the *getting the touch location* section, delete the code from the touchBegan method. You are going to implement a drag action on the sprite rather than a tap to move. This will use the full touch life cycle.

1. Add a new Boolean property to your private interface:

   ```
   @interface HelloWorldScene ()
   @property (nonatomic, assign) BOOL dragging;
   @end
   ```

2. Also, delete the code that makes the sprite spin from the init method.

3. Now, add the following code to the touchBegan method:

   ```
   -(void) touchBegan:(UITouch *)touch withEvent:(UIEvent *)event {
       CGPoint touchLoc = [touch locationInNode:self];

       if (CGRectContainsPoint(_sprite.boundingBox, touchLoc)) {
           self.dragging = YES;
           NSLog(@"Start dragging");
       }
   }
   ```

4. Add a touchMoved method with the following code:

   ```
   - (void)touchMoved:(UITouch *)touch withEvent:(UIEvent *)event {
       CGPoint touchLoc = [touch locationInNode:self];

       if (self.dragging) {
           _sprite.position = touchLoc;
       }
   }
   ```

5. What is being done in these methods is that first you check to see whether the initial touch was inside the sprite. If it was, you set a Boolean to say that the user is dragging the node. It has, in effect, picked up the node.

6. Next, in the touch moved method, it is as simple as if the user did touch down on the node and set the new position of the node to the touch location.

7. Then, you just have to let go of the sprite. This is done in `touchEnded`.

8. Implement the `touchEnded` method as follows:

```
- (void)touchEnded:(UITouch *)touch withEvent:(UIEvent *)event {
    self.dragging = NO;
}
```

9. Now, if you build and run the app, you will be able to drag around the sprite. There is one small problem; if you don't grab the sprite in its center, you will see that the node snaps its center to the touch. What you really want is to just move from the location on the node where it was touched. You will make this adjustment now.

10. To make this fix, you are going to have to calculate the offset on the initial touch from the nodes center point. This will be stored and applied to the final position of the node in `touchMoved`.

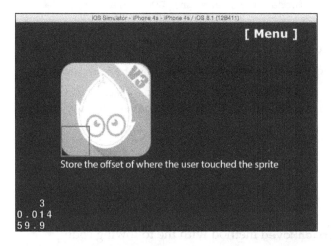

Store the offset of where the user touched the sprite

11. Add another property to your private interface:

```
@property (nonatomic, assign) CGPoint dragOffset;
```

12. Modify your `touchBegan` method to the following code:

```
-(void) touchBegan:(UITouch *)touch withEvent:(UIEvent *)event {
    CGPoint touchLoc = [touch locationInNode:self];
    CGPoint touchOffset = [touch locationInNode:_sprite];

    if (CGRectContainsPoint(_sprite.boundingBox, touchLoc)) {
        self.dragging = YES;
        NSLog(@"Start dragging");
        self.dragOffset = touchOffset;
    }
}
```

Notice that using the `locationInNode` method, you can calculate the position of the touch relative to the node. This information is only useful if the touch was indeed inside the node; so, you only store it if this is the case.

13. Now, modify your `touchMoved` method to the following code:

```
- (void)touchMoved:(UITouch *)touch withEvent:(UIEvent *)event {
    CGPoint touchLoc = [touch locationInNode:self];
    //Check if we are already dragging
    if (self.dragging) {
        CGPoint offsetPosition = ccpSub(touchLoc, self.
dragOffset);
//Calculate an offset to account for the anchor point
CGPoint anchorPointOffset = CGPointMake(_sprite.anchorPoint.x *
_sprite.boundingBox.size.width, _sprite.anchorPoint.y * _sprite.
boundingBox.size.height);
//Add the offset and anchor point adjustment together to get the
final position
        CGPoint positionWithAnchorPoint = ccpAdd(offsetPosition,
anchorPointOffset);
        _sprite.position = positionWithAnchorPoint;
    }
}
```

The offset position is subtracted from the touch location using the Cocos2d convenience function: `ccpSub`. It subtracts a point from another point.

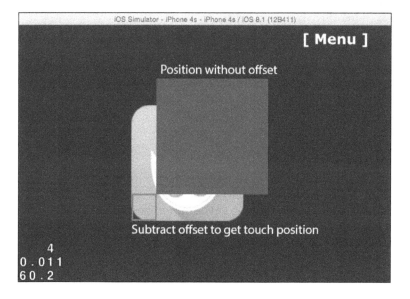

14. Using the anchor point and size of the sprite, an adjustment is calculated to account for different anchor points.

15. Once these two points have been calculated, they are added together to create a final sprite position.

16. Build and run the app now, you will now have a very natural dragging mechanic.

For reference, here are the relevant parts of `HelloWorldScene.m`:

```
@interface HelloWorldScene ()

@property (nonatomic, assign) BOOL dragging;
@property (nonatomic, assign) CGPoint dragOffset;

@end
- (id)init
{
    // Apple recommend assigning self with supers return value
    self = [super init];
    if (!self) return(nil);

    // Enable touch handling on scene node
    self.userInteractionEnabled = YES;

    // Create a colored background (Dark Grey)
    CCNodeColor *background = [CCNodeColor nodeWithColor:[CCColor
colorWithRed:0.2f green:0.2f blue:0.2f alpha:1.0f]];
    [self addChild:background];

    // Add a sprite
    _sprite = [CCSprite spriteWithImageNamed:@"Icon-72.png"];
    _sprite.position  = ccp(self.contentSize.width/2,self.contentSize.
height/2);
    _sprite.anchorPoint = ccp(0.5, 0.5);
    [self addChild:_sprite];

    // Create a back button
    CCButton *backButton = [CCButton buttonWithTitle:@"[ Menu ]"
fontName:@"Verdana-Bold" fontSize:18.0f];
    backButton.positionType = CCPositionTypeNormalized;
    backButton.position = ccp(0.85f, 0.95f); // Top Right of screen
    [backButton setTarget:self selector:@selector(onBackClicked:)];
    [self addChild:backButton];
```

```objc
    // done
    return self;
}
// -----------------------------------------------------------------
-----
#pragma mark - Touch Handler
// -----------------------------------------------------------------
-----

-(void) touchBegan:(UITouch *)touch withEvent:(UIEvent *)event {
    CGPoint touchLoc = [touch locationInNode:self];
    CGPoint touchOffset = [touch locationInNode:_sprite];

    if (CGRectContainsPoint(_sprite.boundingBox, touchLoc)) {
        self.dragging = YES;
        NSLog(@"Start dragging");
        self.dragOffset = touchOffset;
    }
}

- (void)touchMoved:(UITouch *)touch withEvent:(UIEvent *)event {
    CGPoint touchLoc = [touch locationInNode:self];

    if (self.dragging) {
        CGPoint offsetPosition = ccpSub(touchLoc, self.dragOffset);
        CGPoint anchorPointOffset = CGPointMake(_sprite.anchorPoint.x
* _sprite.boundingBox.size.width, _sprite.anchorPoint.y * _sprite.
boundingBox.size.height);
        CGPoint positionWithAnchorPoint = ccpAdd(offsetPosition,
anchorPointOffset);
        _sprite.position = positionWithAnchorPoint;
    }
}

- (void)touchEnded:(UITouch *)touch withEvent:(UIEvent *)event {
    self.dragging = NO;
}
```

Adding buttons to your scene

Buttons are a requirement for almost any app. You will have to use them constantly in your game development. Cocos2d v3 makes this very simple with the introduction of the new class, CCButton. This is a great improvement over version 2 for those familiar with it. Making buttons is now as easy as making any other node. It is even better as they support block-based callbacks or target/selector calls that gives you the flexibility to work with buttons however you like.

Buttons have three states:

- Default
- Selected
- Disabled

If you open up `IntroScene.m` in your Xcode project, you will see an example of a button being created:

```
// Helloworld scene button
CCButton *helloWorldButton = [CCButton buttonWithTitle:@"[ Start ]" fontName:@"Verdana-Bold" fontSize:18.0f];
helloWorldButton.positionType = CCPositionTypeNormalized;
helloWorldButton.position = ccp(0.5f, 0.35f);
[helloWorldButton setTarget:self selector:@selector(onSpinningClicked:)];
[self addChild:helloWorldButton];
```

Buttons are created with either a text-based title or an image. To create a button with an image instead of text, you can use the following code:

```
(id) buttonWithTitle:(NSString*) title spriteFrame:(CCSpriteFrame*) spriteFrame highlightedSpriteFrame:(CCSpriteFrame*) highlighted disabledSpriteFrame:(CCSpriteFrame*) disabled;
```

This method gives you the option of providing an image for all states of a button.

To set a block instead of target/selector is as simple as the following code:

```
[helloWorldButton setBlock:^(id sender) {
    NSLog(@"Button tapped");
}];
```

Accepting user input with form elements

There are many other user input methods that are not buttons. Cocos2d v3 brings a whole suite of form components that were missing from previous versions.

It is also possible to include **UIKit** components, but in nearly all cases, a better user experience will be provided by using the Cocos2d equivalent.

The form elements available are as follows:

- CCButton
- CCTextField
- CCLabelTTF, CCLabelBMFont
- CCSlider
- CCScrollView
- CCTableView

To use these elements, you must provide images for their appearance. However, there is an easier method. SpriteBuilder comes with template versions of the form components and makes their use very simple.

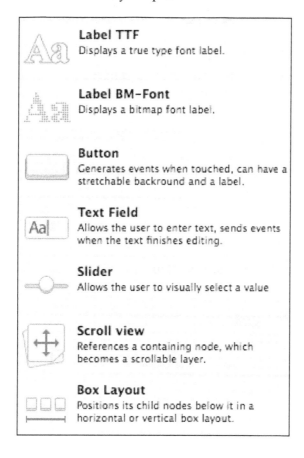

Label TTF
Displays a true type font label.

Label BM-Font
Displays a bitmap font label.

Button
Generates events when touched, can have a stretchable backround and a label.

Text Field
Allows the user to enter text, sends events when the text finishes editing.

Slider
Allows the user to visually select a value

Scroll view
References a containing node, which becomes a scrollable layer.

Box Layout
Positions its child nodes below it in a horizontal or vertical box layout.

These are what each component looks like in an app.

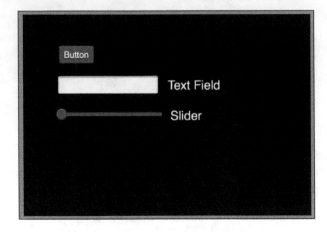

1. Start a new SpriteBuilder project.
2. Drag out some form elements onto the screen and then publish it in Xcode. In order to use these form elements you have placed, you will need to set up code connections.
3. Open the Xcode project for your SpriteBuilder project, and then open the `MainScene.m` file.
4. Add a private interface with some properties for the form elements:
   ```
   @interface MainScene ()
   @property (nonatomic, strong) CCTextField *textField;
   @property (nonatomic, strong) CCSlider *slider;
   @end
   ```
5. Add the **Code Connections** node in SpriteBuilder to match these properties:

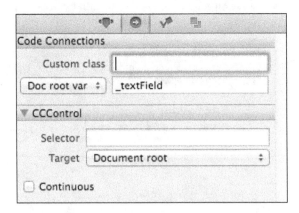

As both `CCSlider` and `CCTextField` are subclasses of `CCControl`, they both support `target/selector` or block-based callbacks. The thing you need to know is when these callbacks are called.

- ° For `CCTextField`, it is when the user presses the return key and the control resigns its first responder status
- ° For `CCSlider`, it is on touch up after the user has changed a value

6. Implement the following `onEnter` method in `MainScene.m` to test this out:

```
- (void)onEnter {
    [super onEnter];

    [self.slider setBlock:^(id sender) {
        NSLog(@"Slider");
    }];

    [self.textField setBlock:^(id sender) {
        NSLog(@"Text field");
    }];
}
```

7. Build and run your app; you should see console output when releasing your touch on the slider or when pressing return on the text field.

Presenting data in a table with CCTableView

The `CCTableView` node is the Cocos2d equivalent of `UITableView`. It can be used in your game whenever you need to present a scrollable list of items such as a high score table. It works a lot like `UITableView`, where a data source provides the instance of the cell to show on screen. In order to learn how to use `CCTableView`, you will create a simple mocked up high score screen. The scores will be stubbed out, but could be easily switched for real data if you want to use this implementation in your game.

Start a new Xcode project and delete all the boilerplate code from the `HelloWorldScene.m` file, so you are left with a blank scene. You might want to leave the back button so that you can navigate back to the main menu.

Creating a CCTableView data source

The first step is to create the data source for your table view. This could be done in a separate class, but to keep things simple in this tutorial, your scene will also be the data source. Following are the steps:

1. You will also need some dummy data to present. Add a new property to your interface for an array of scores:

    ```
    @interface HelloWorldScene () <CCTableViewDataSource>
    @property (nonatomic, strong) NSArray *scores;
    @end
    ```

2. In your `init` method, give it some dummy data. In this example, they are strings:

    ```
    self.scores = @[@"5050", @"3500", @"3400", @"2300", @"1100",
    @"500"];
    ```

3. Now that you have some data on the data source, you will need to implement the `CCTableViewDataSource` protocol. This involves implementing the following methods:

    ```
    (CCTableViewCell*) tableView:(CCTableView*)tableView
    nodeForRowAtIndex:(NSUInteger) index;
    - (float) tableView:(CCTableView*)tableView heightForRowAtIndex:(N
    SUInteger) index
    (NSUInteger) tableViewNumberOfRows:(CCTableView*) tableView;
    ```

4. These methods should remind you of `UITableViewDataSource` as the two work in a very similar manner.

5. Add the protocol to your private interface:

    ```
    @interface HelloWorldScene () <CCTableViewDataSource>
    ```

6. Now, create a new section in your code for the methods:

    ```
    #pragma mark - CCTableViewDataSource
    // ----------------------------------------------------------------
    --------


    - (CCTableViewCell*)tableView:(CCTableView *)tableView
    nodeForRowAtIndex:(NSUInteger)index {
        return nil;
    }


    - (NSUInteger)tableViewNumberOfRows:(CCTableView *)tableView {
        return self.scores.count;
    }
    ```

```
- (float) tableView:(CCTableView*)tableView heightForRowAtIndex:(N
SUInteger) index {
    return 50.0f;
}
```

7. For now, our methods are stubbed out.

8. The next thing you are going to do is create the table view cell. Table view cells are simply another node.

9. You can put whatever type of node you would like on them. For this example, you will be adding a color node as a background and a label for the score.

10. Update the nodeAtRowIndex method to the following code:

```
- (CCTableViewCell*)tableView:(CCTableView *)tableView
nodeForRowAtIndex:(NSUInteger)index {
    CGSize cellSize = CGSizeMake(150.0f, 50.0f);

    CCTableViewCell* cell = [CCTableViewCell node];
    cell.contentSize = cellSize;

//Adjust the color of the node to create a gradient like effect
    float colorAdjust = (index / (float)self.scores.count);
    CCNodeColor* colorNode = [CCNodeColor nodeWithColor:[CCColor
colorWithRed:0.1f green:0.1f blue:(0.5f + 0.5f * colorAdjust) ]
width:cellSize.width height:cellSize.height];

//Create the score label and center it in the color node.
    CCLabelTTF *scoreLabel = [CCLabelTTF labelWithString:self.
scores[index] fontName:@"Marker Felt" fontSize:22.0f];
    scoreLabel.position = ccp(colorNode.boundingBox.size.width/2,
colorNode.boundingBox.size.height/2);
    scoreLabel.anchorPoint = ccp(0.5, 0.5);
    [colorNode addChild:scoreLabel];

    [cell addChild:colorNode];
    return cell;
}
```

The color of the Color Node is set to different shades of blue, based on its index. The color node is added as a child of the cell and the score label is a child of the color node. The score label is also centered in the color node. You could design any node you want. It is a good practice to create a subclass for the cell to keep your code clean.

Adding a CCTableView node to the scene

Now that you have your data source created, you need to actually hook it up to a table view. Adding a table view to your scene is as easy as adding any other node. Following are the steps:

1. In your `init` method, add the following code after you set up the `scores` array:

```
CCTableView* table = [CCTableView node];
    table.dataSource = self; // make our class the data source
    table.block = ^(CCTableView* table) {
        NSLog(@"Cell %d was pressed", (int) table.selectedRow);
    };
    [self addChild:table];
```

2. Build and run your app, you should see a scrollable table view for your high scores. Add some more high scores to your array and look at how the table view changes.

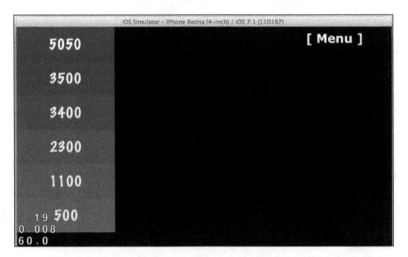

 For reference, the complete code is available in the code bundle provided with the book.

3. If you want to extend this high scores screen, you could perform the following steps:

   ° Instead of taking an array of strings, it would be better to take an array of a custom object. This object could contain a name, score, and date. You would then have to update the design to accommodate these new fields by adding more labels.

   ° You could pass in an array of high scores rather than hard coding it. This would make the high score screen much more portable.

   ° The scene at the moment is a bit bland. You could style it up using SpriteBuilder or in code in order to have a title and a background.

Summary

In this chapter, you learned how to respond to a variety of inputs from the user. You also learned how to detect touches on the screen and how to use these touches to change properties of your nodes. You also learned how to use form elements to accept other types of inputs from users.

In the next chapter, you will learn all about how to use physics in your app. Physics will be used with both SpriteBuilder and code. You will also create an interactive physics-based game to learn these concepts.

6
Physics Engines

These days, most games will use some form of physics in their game play. Be it just to detect collision between objects or to create a more realistic feel to movements within a game. Physics engines can add a great deal of polish to a game without a large amount of effort, and as such it is an important skill to have. Physics takes your game to the next level.

You have already had some exposure to basic physics in the previous chapters. Physics was used to detect collisions in the Flappy Bird-style game and was also used to make your bird move up and down through the scene. There is so much more that can be done with physics and you will learn some of it in this chapter.

This chapter covers the following topics:

- Different physics engine techniques
- Build a simple app that allows you to fire a catapult at a stack of objects
- See how these objects will fall down

It will be similar to how Angry Birds works.

Introducing physics engines

Cocos2d v3 has an inbuilt-integrated physics engine. The physics engine it uses is actually a third-party library named **Chipmunk**. In the previous versions of Cocos2d, there was the option of using either Box2D or Chipmunk as they weren't built into Cocos2d, but simply could be used with Cocos2d. Now, Chipmunk support is built right into Cocos2d, which makes it very easy to use and makes it a simple choice on which engine to use. Following are the steps:

1. Start by creating a new SpriteBuilder project. This app shall be named `Catapult`.

2. Open the project settings and change the default scaling to 2x. Remember this is for the automatic scaling that SpriteBuilder uses when importing assets.

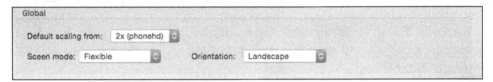

3. Import the catapult assets provided by dragging them into SpriteBuilder. Following are the two assets that will be used to create your catapult:

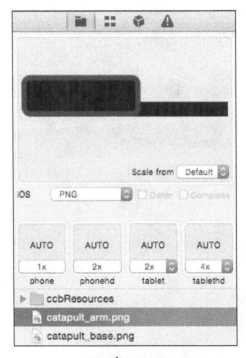

catapult_arm.png

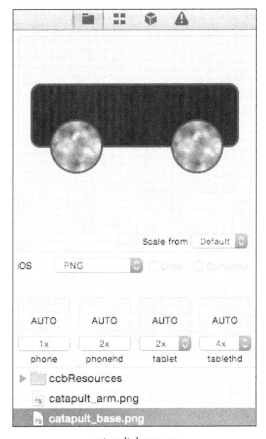

catapult_base.png

4. Delete the template scene and add a new layer so you have more room to work with. Decorate the layer with a gradient node for the sky and a green color node for the ground.

5. Next, add a physics node. Remember from the previous chapters that every object that interacts with physics must be a child of a physics node.

6. Next, drag out the assets for the catapult base and arm as children of the physics node.

7. Set the anchor point of the arm to $(1.0, 0.0)$ so that it rotates around its bottom-right corner.

8. Now, enable physics for both the base and the arm by opening the physics page on the right-hand side of SpriteBuilder and tick **Enable physics**:

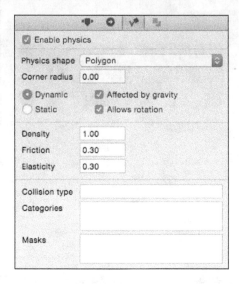

9. Currently, running your app will see the catapult parts quickly falling off the screen. To fix this, you need to enable the ground to also use physics and make it a **Static** object.

10. Make the ground node a child of the physics node and click on **Enable physics** option in the same way as the catapult parts.

11. Running the game now will see the catapult falling apart on launch, but at least it will stay on screen.

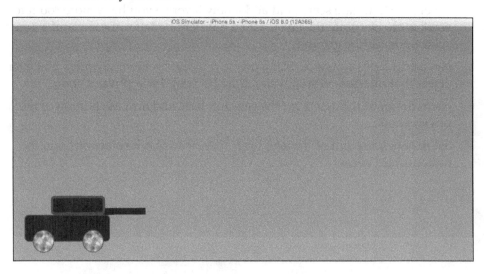

Obviously, your catapult should not fall apart. You need a way to join the two parts together. This leads to the next technique, that is, **joints**.

Adding joints

A joint does exactly what it sounds like it would do. It joins objects together. There are three types of joints:

- **Physics Pivot Joint**: This connects two objects with a single point
- **Physics Distance Joint**: This connects two objects together at a set distance
- **Physics Spring Joint**: This connects two objects together at a set distance, but instead of the joint being rigidly set, it allows the distance to change in the manner of a spring

1. The first step is to make the base of your catapult static. You don't want it to move throughout the scene.

2. The joint you will be using is the first option: the physics pivot joint as you want your catapult arm to pivot around a point.

   All of the physics joints are available in the SpriteBuilder objects pane.

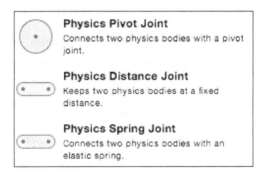

3. Drag **Physics Pivot Joint** onto the scene and position it in the top-right corner of the catapult base.

4. Next, move the catapult arm so that its anchor point sits exactly at the center of the pivot joint. You can also rotate the arm so that it is facing straight up.

Your scene should now look like the following screenshot:

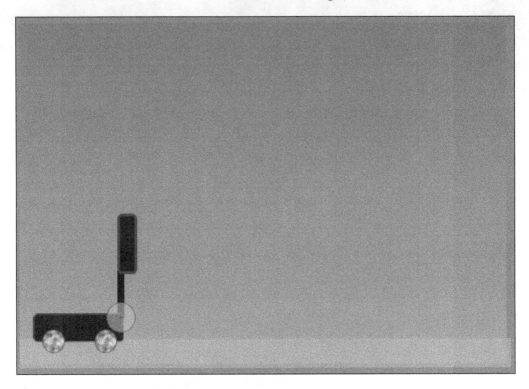

Currently, the joint is not actually joining any objects. Despite the fact that it is sitting on top of the two bodies you want to join together.

5. To set what the joint holds together, you need to edit the properties of the joint in the editor on the right-hand side of SpriteBuilder.

6. Drag the setting out, and select the arm and the base for **Body A** and **Body B**. It should look like the following screenshot when you are done:

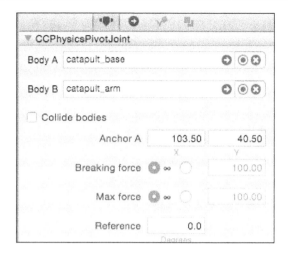

7. Build and run your game now. You should see your catapult no longer falls apart!

Congratulations! you just created your first physics joint.

Adding a sprite joint

Now, the catapult at least holds itself together, but it is not the greatest structure ever created. The arm instantly falls down. What you want is the arm to stay up and then be able to be dragged backwards.

To achieve this behavior, you will use the **Physics Spring Joint**. The question however is what are you joining it to? Perform the following steps:

1. You need to hook up your arm to an invisible object that is above the catapult, which will hold the arm up. As this is a spring, which will allow the arm to be pulled in different directions and spring back.

2. Add a blank CCNode as a child of the physics node. This node will have no size. Click on **Enable physics** for the node and set it to be **Static**.

3. Now, drag out a physics spring node and set the two bodies on the node to be between the invisible node and the catapult arm.

4. Build and run your game; your catapult arm should not fall down now.

You will tune the values of the spring joint later when you can test out the dragging feature. First, you need to implement the dragging feature.

Dragging an object against a spring joint

In order to drag our catapult arm back, we will create another joint. However, this joint will be between our finger and the catapult arm. As you can't create a joint to your finger, what you will do is create another empty node that will move based on touch. This empty node will be joined to the catapult arm. Following are the steps:

1. Create a new empty node as in the last section. Enable physics and set it to static. The position of the node does not matter as it will be moved in code, but you must ensure that it is a child of the physics node. Add a code connection called `_touchNode` to the new node.

2. You will also need a code connection for the catapult arm. Call it `_catapultArm`.

3. Add another code connection for the physics node: `_physicsNode`.

4. You will do this section in code. Switch over to Xcode.

5. First, add the property implementation for your new code connection. Also, add another property for the new joint that will be created in code:

   ```
   @interface MainScene ()

   @property (nonatomic, strong) CCNode *physicsNode;
   @property (nonatomic, strong) CCNode *catapultArm;
   @property (nonatomic, strong) CCNode *touchNode;
   @property (nonatomic, strong) CCPhysicsJoint *touchJoint;

   @end
   ```

6. First, you will need to enable user interaction on the scene. Add the `didLoadFromCCB` method:

   ```
   - (void)didLoadFromCCB {
       self.userInteractionEnabled = YES;

       self.touchNode.physicsBody.collisionMask = @[];
   }
   ```

7. Also in the `didloadfromCCB` method, you are setting the touch node to collide with no other objects. This stops it from getting in the way.

8. Add the following method to `touchBegan`:

   ```
   - (void)touchBegan:(UITouch *)touch withEvent:(UIEvent *)event {
       CGPoint touchLocation = [touch locationInNode:self];

       //Is the touch location in the catapult arm?
   ```

```
    if (CGRectContainsPoint(self.catapultArm.boundingBox,
touchLocation)) {
        //Move the touch node to the position of the touch.
        self.touchNode.position = touchLocation;

        //Attach a spring between the touch node and the catapult
arm
        self.touchJoint = [CCPhysicsJoint connectedSpringJoin
tWithBodyA:self.touchNode.physicsBody bodyB:self.catapultArm.
physicsBody anchorA:ccp(0, 0) anchorB:ccp(15, 15) restLength:0.0f
stiffness:3000.0f damping:150.0f];
    }
}
```

9. What this method does is simple. If the touch begins inside the bounds of the catapult arm, move the touch node to the position of the touch. Next, add a joint between the touch node and the catapult arm.

10. Next, you will need to define the behavior on touch moved:

```
- (void)touchMoved:(UITouch *)touch withEvent:(UIEvent *)event {
    CGPoint touchLocation = [touch locationInNode:self];
    self.touchNode.position = touchLocation;
}
```

11. For this, you are simply moving the touch node position to the new touch location. You don't need to worry about checking the bounds of the catapult arm because the joint will only exist if the touch started within the catapult arm.

12. For `touchEnded` and `touchCancelled` events, you will create a fire catapult method:

```
- (void)touchEnded:(UITouch *)touch withEvent:(UIEvent *)event {
    [self fireCatapult];
}
```

```
- (void)touchCancelled:(UITouch *)touch withEvent:(UIEvent *)event
{
    [self fireCatapult];
}
```

```
- (void)fireCatapult {
    if (self.touchJoint) {
        [self.touchJoint invalidate];
        self.touchJoint = nil;
    }
}
```

13. This method simply destroys the joint. It will allow the spring joint we attached in SpriteBuilder to pull the catapult arm back up.

14. Build and run the app now. You should see the basic behavior; you will need to tune the values of the spring joint in SpriteBuilder until you get something that you like.

    For reference, the values used in the book are:

    ```
    RestLength: 50Dampening: 50Stiffness: 750
    ```

You can also play around with the position of the invisible node and the anchor points of the joints.

Once you have this, you will have a catapult that actually holds itself together and can be fired by dragging it back and letting it go. Wouldn't it be great if you could actually fire something out of the catapult though?

Firing objects from the catapult

You will now learn how to launch an object from the catapult. This will be accomplished by combining techniques into one smooth action, which you have already learned. Following are the steps:

1. The first step to firing an object from the catapult is to actually make an object.

2. Open SpriteBuilder and add a new node named `Brick`. Set bricks size to be (`25`, `25`) and its anchor point to be (`0.5`, `0.5`). Enable physics and set its density to a high value such as 50.0, and its friction to be 1.0, and its elasticity to 0.

3. Add a color node to the node and give it an orange color to make it look more like a brick.

4. Publish and switch back to Xcode.

5. In order to fire an object, you will use the same techniques that you have already used. When the user touches down on the catapult arm, you will add a new object to it. You will then connect it to the arm with a pivot joint. Once the catapult is released, you will invalidate this joint and let the brick fly.

6. First modify the interface to add two new properties:

   ```
   @property (nonatomic, strong) CCNode *brick;
   @property (nonatomic, strong) CCPhysicsJoint *brickJoint;
   ```

   These will be used to keep track of your brick when it is being used.

7. Next, modify the `touchBegan` method in the following code:

```
- (void)touchBegan:(UITouch *)touch withEvent:(UIEvent *)event {
    CGPoint touchLocation = [touch locationInNode:self];

    //Is the touch location in the catapult arm?
    if (CGRectContainsPoint(self.catapultArm.boundingBox,
touchLocation)) {
        //Move the touch node to the position of the touch.
        self.touchNode.position = touchLocation;

        //Attach a spring between the touch node and the catapult
arm
        self.touchJoint = [CCPhysicsJoint connectedSpringJoin
tWithBodyA:self.touchNode.physicsBody bodyB:self.catapultArm.
physicsBody anchorA:ccp(0, 0) anchorB:ccp(15, 15) restLength:0.0f
stiffness:3000.0f damping:150.0f];

        //Setup the brick
        CCNode *brick = [CCBReader load:@"Brick"];
        CGPoint brickPosition = [self.catapultArm
convertToWorldSpace:ccp(35, 35)];
        brick.position = brickPosition;
        [self.physicsNode addChild:brick];
        self.brick.physicsBody.collisionMask = @[];
        self.brick.physicsBody.allowsRotation = NO;
        self.brick = brick;

        self.brickJoint = [CCPhysicsJoint connectedPivotJointW
ithBodyA:brick.physicsBody bodyB:self.catapultArm.physicsBody
anchorA:ccp(15, 15)];
    }
}
```

This adds a new brick to the scene and sets up its position. You will notice that rotation and collision have been disabled. This is to avoid weird behavior when the brick is in the catapult. Once it is released, these will be enabled again.

8. Now that you have added the brick to the catapult arm, you just need to release it.

9. Modify your fire catapult method to the following code:

```
- (void) fireCatapult {
    if (self.touchJoint) {
        [self.touchJoint invalidate];
        self.touchJoint = nil;

        [self.brickJoint invalidate];
        self.brickJoint = nil;

        self.brick.physicsBody.collisionMask = nil;
        self.brick.physicsBody.allowsRotation = YES;
    }
}
```

This should look very familiar by now. You invalidate the joint, and also the renewable collisions and rotation for the brick.

10. Build and run your app. You should now be able to throw bricks from your catapult!

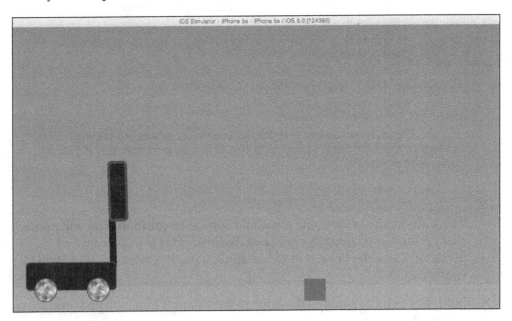

11. Now all you need to do is build something to destroy.

12. Open SpriteBuilder and drag out some color nodes to create a structure of your choice.

13. Make sure they are all children of the physics node and then enable physics on all of them. Give them a solid weight so they don't go flying too far (unless that's what you want!).

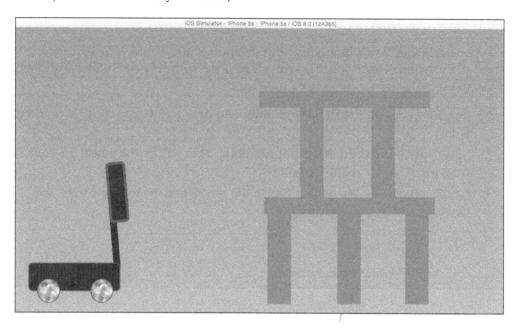

14. Build and run your game when your structure is complete. Enjoy knocking it down.

Creating a motor

A great feature of joints is that they can be turned into a motor. A joint can be given a rate of rotation that can be used to propel objects through the scene. This can be used to add objects that behave like vehicles in your game.

To demonstrate this, you will modify your catapult to drive into your structure instead of throwing objects at it. This can all be done within SpriteBuilder. Following are the steps:

1. Open up your project in SpriteBuilder and drag out a `CCColorNode` onto the scene.

2. Make sure it is a child of the physics node. This will be the wheel for your catapult, so resize it appropriately.

3. Enable physics on the node. Change the physics shape to be a **Circle**, the density to `10.00`, and the friction to `1.00`.

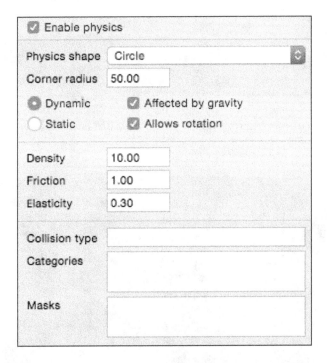

4. Position your wheel node in roughly the position of the back wheel.

5. Drag out a **Physics Pin Joint** and pin the catapult to the back wheel. Your scene should now look like the following screenshot:

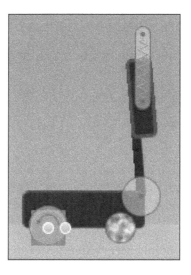

6. To turn the pivot joint into a motor is as simple as clicking a tick box. In the settings for the **Pivot Joint** on the right-hand side of the screen is a **Motor** section. Enable the motor and set its rate to **10.00**.

7. To free your cart, you can also delete the spring joint that is holding up the catapult arm.

8. Publish your scene and open it in Xcode. Build and run the project.

You should now see your cart driving ahead. It drags its front side along the ground as it does not have any wheel object.

See whether you can use the same techniques to add a wheel in the front.

The next step

If you would like to explore physics some more, here are some ideas:

- Create a car game where you have to drive over the hills
- Tie the rate of the motor joint to the touch of the screen in order to give control to the user
- Add targets to shoot at objects. You can use collisions to detect whether the target was hit

Summary

Congratulations! You have just built a physics sample project. Using these techniques, you can build an endless supply of physics-based games.

You learned how to enable physics on objects so they are affected by gravity. You also learned how to join objects together with one of three types of joints: Pivot joints, Distance joints, and Spring joints.

You learned how to use touch to interact with the physics world. You then learned how to turn joints into motors to enable more possibilities.

Index

K

keyframe animation
creating 75-77

M

main editor window, SpriteBuilder 46
MenuScene class
adding 38-40
motor
creating 114, 115
move animations
creating 78-80
multiple coordinate systems
working with 23

N

nodes
about 17-20
children nodes 20
content size types 20
position types 20

O

Objective-C 7
onEnter method 35
onEnterTransitionDidFinish method 35
onExit method 35
onExitTransitionDidStart method 35
options pane, SpriteBuilder 48

P

particle systems
about 61, 69, 70
coding 74
designing 73
particle systems, modes
Gravity 71
Radial 71
particle systems, properties
Angle 71
Duration 70
Emit Rate 70

End Color 71
End Size 71
End Spin 71
Life 70
Mode 70
Position Variance 70
Start Color 71
Start Size 71
Start Spin 71
Total Particles 70
Physics Distance Joint 105
physics engines
about 102
Catapult app, creating 102-105
Physics Pivot Joint 105
Physics Spring Joint 105
popScene method 38
popToRootScene method 38
position property 18
position types, nodes
Normalized 20
Points 20
UI Points 20
pushScene method 37

R

Radial mode, properties
End Radius 72
Rotate 72
Start Radius 72
replaceScene method 37
resource pane, SpriteBuilder 47
rotate animations
creating 78-80

S

scale animations
creating 78-80
scene
about 35
buttons, adding 91, 92
CCScene, creating 37
CCTableView, adding 98, 99
life cycle 35-37

Thank you for buying
Cocos2D Game Development Essentials

About Packt Publishing

Packt, pronounced 'packed', published its first book, *Mastering phpMyAdmin for Effective MySQL Management*, in April 2004, and subsequently continued to specialize in publishing highly focused books on specific technologies and solutions.

Our books and publications share the experiences of your fellow IT professionals in adapting and customizing today's systems, applications, and frameworks. Our solution-based books give you the knowledge and power to customize the software and technologies you're using to get the job done. Packt books are more specific and less general than the IT books you have seen in the past. Our unique business model allows us to bring you more focused information, giving you more of what you need to know, and less of what you don't.

Packt is a modern yet unique publishing company that focuses on producing quality, cutting-edge books for communities of developers, administrators, and newbies alike. For more information, please visit our website at www.packtpub.com.

About Packt Open Source

In 2010, Packt launched two new brands, Packt Open Source and Packt Enterprise, in order to continue its focus on specialization. This book is part of the Packt Open Source brand, home to books published on software built around open source licenses, and offering information to anybody from advanced developers to budding web designers. The Open Source brand also runs Packt's Open Source Royalty Scheme, by which Packt gives a royalty to each open source project about whose software a book is sold.

Writing for Packt

We welcome all inquiries from people who are interested in authoring. Book proposals should be sent to author@packtpub.com. If your book idea is still at an early stage and you would like to discuss it first before writing a formal book proposal, then please contact us; one of our commissioning editors will get in touch with you.

We're not just looking for published authors; if you have strong technical skills but no writing experience, our experienced editors can help you develop a writing career, or simply get some additional reward for your expertise.

Creating Games with cocos2d for iPhone 2

ISBN: 978-1-84951-900-7   Paperback: 388 pages

Master cocos2d through building nine complete games for the iPhone

1. Games are explained in detail, from the design decisions to the code itself.

2. Learn to build a wide variety of game types, from a memory tile game to an endless runner.

3. Use different design approaches to help you explore the cocos2d framework.

Cocos2d-X by Example Beginner's Guide

ISBN: 978-1-78216-734-1   Paperback: 246 pages

Make fun games for any platform using C++, combined with one of the most popular open source frameworks in the world

1. Learn to build multi-device games in simple, easy steps, letting the framework do all the heavy lifting.

2. Spice things up in your games with easy to apply animations, particle effects, and physics simulation.

3. Quickly implement and test your own gameplay ideas, with an eye for optimization and portability.

Please check **www.PacktPub.com** for information on our titles

Learning iPhone Game Development with Cocos2D 3.0

ISBN: 978-1-78216-014-4   Paperback: 434 pages

Harness the power of Cocos2D to create your own stunning and engaging games for iOS

1. Find practical solutions to many real-world game development problems.

2. Create games from start to finish by writing code and following detailed step-by-step instructions.

3. Full of illustrations and diagrams, practical examples, and tips for deeper understanding of game development in Cocos2D for iPhone.

Cocos2d for iPhone 1 Game Development Cookbook

ISBN: 978-1-84951-400-2   Paperback: 446 pages

Over 90 recipes for iOS 2D game development using cocos2d

1. Discover advanced Cocos2d, OpenGL ES, and iOS techniques spanning all areas of the game development process.

2. Learn how to create top-down isometric games, side-scrolling platformers, and games with realistic lighting.

3. Full of fun and engaging recipes with modular libraries that can be plugged into your project.

Please check **www.PacktPub.com** for information on our titles